30 Days to Market Mastery

Founded in 1807, John Wiley & Sons is the oldest independent publishing company in the United States. With offices in North America, Europe, Australia and Asia, Wiley is globally committed to developing and marketing print and electronic products and services for our customers' professional and personal knowledge and understanding.

The Wiley Trading series features books by traders who have survived the market's ever-changing temperament and have prospered—some by reinventing systems, others by getting back to basics. Whether a novice trader, professional or somewhere in between, these books will provide the advice and strategies needed to prosper today and well into the future.

For a list of available titles, visit our Web site at www.WileyFinance.com.

30 Days to Market Mastery

A Step-by-Step Guide to Profitable Trading

JACOB BERNSTEIN

John Wiley & Sons, Inc.

Published by John Wiley & Sons, Inc., Hoboken, New Jersey.
Published simultaneously in Canada.

Wiley Bicentennial Logo: Richard J. Pacifico

Library of Congress Cataloging-in-Publication Data:

Bernstein, Jacob, 1946–
30 days to market mastery : a step by step guide to profitable trading /
Jake Bernstein.
p. cm. – (Wiley trading series)
Includes index.
ISBN 978-0-470-10987-8 (cloth)
1. Futures. 2. Futures market–Examinations, questions, etc. I. Title.
II. Title: Thirty days to market mastery.
HG024.A3B4748 2007
332.64′52–dc22

2006036782

Printed in the United States of America.

10 9 8 7 6 5 4 3 2 1

Contents

Preface

Living in a capitalist society provides us with numerous opportunities and methods by which we can multiply our money. As capitalism slowly—but ever so surely—continues its seemingly inevitable advance to all countries in the world, investment opportunities grow as well. We no longer live in a world of disconnected economies; rather we live in a world of intricately intertwined and interdependent economies. A change in Chinese interest rates reverberates throughout the financial world, impacting stock and commodity markets as well as foreign currency relationships. A potential banking problem in Russia sends shock waves across all market sectors as stocks in the United States reflect the possible impact of the news. OPEC ministers agree to cut oil production by a larger than expected amount and prices in the crude oil futures pits surge higher. Stocks on major world exchanges drop on fears of inflation due to increased oil prices and interest rate futures drop sharply in response to concerns that inflationary pressures may cause central banks to raise interest rates. At the same time, gold and silver futures push higher as investors rush to buy these inflation sensitive markets.

Volatility and large daily price swings have become the norm as international economic growth and market participation have expanded. While the opportunities provided by volatility have opened the door to huge profits, they have also brought with them substantial and heretofore unheard of risks. This has caused many individual investors and traders in stocks and commodities to withdraw from the markets for fear that they may lack either the expertise and/or the risk tolerance to participate in the developing market moves.

Many investors have, therefore, chosen to entrust their hard-earned money to the supposedly capable hands of professional money managers. They have enlisted the assistance of investment bankers, financial planners, hedge funds pension fund or retirement fund managers, mutual funds or more conservative investment managers who use such vehicles as corporate bonds or government issued treasury securities as their preferred investment areas. Unfortunately, many of us have been disappointed by the experts. All too often the cost of having our money professionally managed is too high given the seemingly low returns. In recent years, some professionally managed programs—in particular hedge funds—have actually lost money for their clients.

If you have ever looked at the performance of your investments and said, "I could do better," it is very possible that you are right. With the right tools, sufficient money, motivation, persistence, and consistency, I believe that many individuals can do just as well or even better than some professional money managers. I believe that this holds true for the futures markets as well as the stock markets. I believe that you can do it on your own and that you do not need a degree in finance, banking or economics to achieve your goals of financial freedom. In fact, too much education and knowledge in finance could prove to be a detriment to making money in the markets.

The lessons presented in this book are designed to take you to a level that will facilitate your chances of success in the futures markets. This is not to say that futures trading is without risk. Futures trading is, in fact, the riskiest game in town. My goal is to reduce the risk and increase the odds of success using solid tools that I have developed over the last 35 years. But the tools presented here are not applicable to futures trading alone. Most of them are equally applicable to stocks. Hopefully, you will learn tools that will assist you for many years to come whether you're a commodity or stock investor.

ORGANIZATION

Although the 22 lessons that follow can be completed in 30 days time, you may want to take longer with your studies. Lessons 1 through 15 can be completed in the first 15 days. Take longer with lessons 16 through 18. (I suggest two days for each.) Lessons 19 and 20 should be given three days each. Give Lesson 21 one day and spend two days or more on Lesson 22. In all, the process can be completed in 30 days but, of course, you are advised to move at your own pace.

ANSWERS TO QUIZZES

I have provided a quiz at the end of all but two of the lessons. You can get the answers at my Internet Web site at the http://www.trade-futures.com/30DaysKey.html. I can be reached by e-mail at jake@trade-futures.com.

Acknowledgments

The following people and organizations provided me with the highest caliber of assistance in the completion of this project. I thank all of them for their efforts, encouragement, input, support, and help.

- Emilie Herman at John Wiley & Sons was a pure pleasure to have worked with on this project. She made me look good.
- Lynn Doherty, at my office, spent many hours organizing, reorganizing, and reformatting my charts and tests. I thank her for her assistance.
- To my wife, Linda, I give thanks for the hours I borrowed from our time together.
- Thanks to my office staff for screening phone calls and helping me make time for this project.
- My right-hand associate and organizer, Marilyn Kinney, who has been with me for over 30 years and through every one of my books, knows well by now how to keep me on course for my deadlines, and I thank her deeply.
- To Kevin Commins at John Wiley & Sons, who gave me the opportunity to write yet another book for Wiley, I extend thanks!
- Finally, the very good people at Genesis Financial Technologies (http://www.genesisft.com) are owed a very special word of thanks for providing the outstanding charting and analysis software that helped make this book, my research, and my trading possible.

Introduction

Financial markets throughout the world have changed their nature and structure dramatically since the 1970s. High-speed computers, powerful analytical software, the declining cost of commissions, instantaneous communications via the Internet, rapid dissemination of financially related news, business radio and television, the emergence of second- and third-world powers as significant financial and monetary forces, and the growing world dependence on fossil fuel have all combined in one grand "machine" to change the face of the markets. Events that affect the Chinese currency can and will have a ripple effect on currencies and markets the world over. Stock prices can be influenced dramatically by trends in underlying commodity prices. Daily price volatility has exploded in virtually every sector of the financial markets. This has created more opportunity *as well as* more risk. It has also narrowed the differences between stock and commodity markets. Indeed, in recent years there has been a growing participation by hedge funds, pension funds, and investment companies in the commodity markets.

The search for effective and consistent trading information has taken traders in many directions, some productive, most of them dead ends. My goal in this course is to give you some solid tools that you can implement into your trading plan whether in stocks, commodities, or both. I have provided examples of my methods in stocks as well as in commodities. Some methods are exclusively geared to commodities; however, most are applicable to both. In the event that you have questions, comments or corrections please e-mail me: jake@trade-futures.com.

Jake Bernstein
Highland Park, Illinois
September 2006

LESSON 1, DAY 1

The Structure of a Trade

INTRODUCTION

The stock and futures markets have several functions. In stocks, the market allows corporations to raise funds for expansion of their businesses. In futures, the most important function is to provide a means by which producers—such as farmers, mining companies, banks, and the like—and end users—such as manufacturers, food processors, petroleum processors, and the like—can market what they produce and buy what they need. By far these two groups of market participants comprise most of the transactions that occur in futures. However, the third major group, traders or investors, provide a buffer between the two major groups and also constitute a good portion of market activity.

Figure 1.1 shows the general structure of futures market participants and their orientation to the markets. This model does not apply to the stock market, where the structure is not as complicated.

THE PURPOSE OF TRADING OR INVESTING

As speculators or traders, we have only one purpose or goal in trading and that is to make money. *There is no other goal!*

If you are in the futures markets for any other reason, then you are doing this for the *wrong* reason.

Producers	Traders/Investors	End Users
Farmers	Short-term traders	Grain processors
Mining companies	Day traders	Petroleum "crackers"
Banks	Pit brokers	Food processors
Petroleum companies	Hedge funds	Meat processors
Money managers	Money managers	Banks and mortgage companies
Mortgage companies		
Can be buyers or sellers, but are primarily sellers for the purpose of locking in a profit	Can be buyers, sellers or on both sides using spreads (to be explained)	Are primarily buyers because they need the product in order to run their businesses but they can also be sellers at times

FIGURE 1.1 Futures market participants.

THE PURPOSE OF THIS COURSE

The purpose of this lesson is:

- To teach you the specific structure you will need in order to trade the futures markets objectively.
- To give you a solid education in the most effective way to structure a trade.
- To teach you trading tools and methods that are 100 percent objective and that eliminate vague decisions and unclear trading signals.
- To show you several methods of proper risk management.
- To elucidate and emphasize the *major* importance of profit maximizing strategies.
- To provide you with the proper organizational, analytical, and behavioral skills that are vital to consistent success in trading.

Without the proper structure for a trade, you have nothing!

If you truly want to succeed, then you need to structure every single trade correctly. If you do not, then you will likely lose money—and if you make money, then it will be out of sheer dumb luck. Making money by chance is a hit or miss proposition that does not bring lasting success. Furthermore, it does not teach you anything. If that is how you want to trade or invest, then you might as well buy a lottery ticket. Your chances of making money are about the same as they are if you trade without the proper structure.

WHAT IS "STRUCTURE"?

Every trade *must* have three aspects to it. These three aspects, or steps, comprise the structure of a trade. Structure in trading is necessary because it decreases the odds of random or emotional decisions and it brings vital organization to your trading. The three steps are:

1. **Setup,** which consists of a high probability repetitive pattern.
2. **Trigger,** which confirms or puts into motion a setup.
3. **Follow-through,** which is the method used to minimize losses and, most important of all, to maximize profits.

Now let's define each of these more specifically.

STEP 1: DETERMINE A SETUP

As noted above, a setup (*S*) is a pattern that has shown a strong tendency to repeat over time. There are literally thousands of setups, but few are reliable or accurate.

The following are examples of setups:

- Chart patterns such as gaps, pennants, head-and-shoulders, support, resistance, flags, trend lines, reversals, key reversals, island tops, and bottoms
- Formations such as Gann, Elliott, Fibonacci, regression line analysis
- Cycles, seasonals, ratios, anniversary dates

The first setups I will teach you are based on seasonal key dates. This method is highly reliable and constitutes one of the most effective approaches that I know of to futures and stock trading. Table 1.1 is an example of a key date seasonal setup.

As you can see, this setup or pattern has a *very specific* set of rules. It is totally objective. It is not a matter of opinion, a theory, or an assumption. It is an exact statement of history. The vast majority of traders use market entry and exit methods that have never been tested. They have no idea of how often their methods have been correct. They believe what they have read in a book or heard from another trader. *This is where and how the methods that I teach you differ dramatically from what you may now be using or what you may have heard elsewhere.*

TABLE 1.1 Example: A Key Date Seasonal Setup

Long May Crude Light		Enter: 1/27	Exit: 2/2	Stop %: 4.00	P/L Ratio: 6.0	Trade # 92541921
Contract Year	**Date In**	**Price In**	**Date Out**	**Price Out**	**Profit/Loss**	**Total**
1984	27-Jan	29.68	2-Feb	29.82	0.14	0.14
1985	28-Jan	24.86	4-Feb	25.93	1.07	1.21
1986	27-Jan	20.75	29-Jan	19.79	−0.96	0.25
1987	27-Jan	18.17	2-Feb	18.3	0.13	0.38
1988	27-Jan	16.58	2-Feb	16.75	0.17	0.55
1989	27-Jan	16.87	2-Feb	17.14	0.27	0.82
1990	29-Jan	21.56	2-Feb	21.94	0.38	1.2
1991	28-Jan	19.51	4-Feb	19.52	0.01	1.21
1992	27-Jan	19.49	3-Feb	19.24	−0.25	0.96
1993	27-Jan	19.8	2-Feb	20.07	0.27	1.23
1994	27-Jan	15.46	2-Feb	15.99	0.53	1.76
1995	27-Jan	17.8	2-Feb	18.13	0.33	2.09
1996	29-Jan	17.04	2-Feb	17.19	0.15	2.24
1997	27-Jan	22.98	3-Feb	23.25	0.27	2.51
1998	27-Jan	17.35	2-Feb	17.42	0.07	2.58
1999	27-Jan	12.47	2-Feb	12.53	0.06	2.64
2000	27-Jan	25.58	2-Feb	25.96	0.38	3.02
2001	29-Jan	27.65	2-Feb	29.61	1.96	4.98
2002	28-Jan	20.48	4-Feb	20.56	0.08	5.06
2003	27-Jan	30.49	3-Feb	31.34	0.85	5.91
2004	27-Jan	32.61	2-Feb	32.75	0.14	6.05
Trades:		Winners:	Losers:		% Winners:	Daily PF:
21		19	2		90.48	0.0636
Avg Prof:		Avg Loss:	% Avg Prof:		% Avg Loss:	
0.3821		−0.605	1.66		−2.95	

What does the setup above tell us? It tells us that buying May crude oil futures on the close of trading January 27 and exiting February 2 (or on the close of business the next trading day if the market is closed on the given date) would have been correct over 90 percent of the time since 1984 using a stop-loss close of only 4 percent below the entry price.

Note that this is only a setup. It is *not* a call to action. It is only the first step. Even though this is a potentially excellent trade, we need to go to step 2, which is the trigger.

STEP 2: USE A TRIGGER FOR EVERY SETUP

The *trigger* is a method used to confirm or validate a setup. The methods you will learn in this course require a *setup* and a trigger for every trade. *There are no exceptions to this rule!*

Triggers are similar to what most traders call timing indicators. The triggers I teach you are very simple and very specific. Remember, it is the combination of setup and trigger that places you way ahead of most traders.

In future lessons, you will learn specific combinations of setups and triggers that work well together.

STEP 3: EVERY SETUP AND TRIGGER COMBINATION MUST HAVE A FOLLOW-THROUGH METHOD

The follow-through method is designed to:

- Manage and/or limit the risk
- Maximize profits

Without both elements, you will likely be like most traders—you will have many small victories that will be more than neutralized by a number of large losses. Unless you are able to bank large profits, you will never succeed at this game.

In future lessons, you will learn specific follow-through methods designed to limit losses and maximize profits.

REVIEW

In this lesson, you learned the basic structure of each trade. The structure of every trade consists of three elements:

1. Setup
2. Trigger
3. Follow-through

Some specific examples were given.

Please take a few minutes to answer the questions below.

LESSON 1 QUIZ

Instructions: Circle the correct answers.

1. The three major groups of participants in the futures markets are:

   A. Buyers, sellers, and speculators.
   B. Speculators, producers, and end users.
   C. Winners, losers, and spread traders.
   D. Setups, triggers, and follow-throughs.

2. A setup is:

   A. A bad tip given to you by a broker.
   B. A winning trade.
   C. A losing trade.
   D. A pattern that repeats over time.

3. A trigger is:

   A. A trade that has over 90 percent probability of being correct.
   B. A market that makes large moves based on weather.
   C. The trading system used by all successful speculators.
   D. A method that validates or confirms a setup.

4. Follow-through:

   A. Consists of risk management and profit maximizing strategies.
   B. Is not necessary in cases of 90 percent odds.
   C. Is used only by losing traders.
   D. Consists of three moving averages.

5. For our purposes the goal of futures trading is:

   A. To help your children through college.
   B. To help brokers generate more commissions.
   C. To learn new systems and methods of trading.
   D. To make money.

6. End users in the futures markets:

   A. Are primarily buyers.
   B. Always trade commodity spreads.

C. Are generally uneducated in futures trading methods.

D. Take advantage of small traders.

7. Proper structure of every trade is:

A. Necessary since it decreases the odds of random or emotional decisions.

B. An effective way of taking delivery on futures contracts.

C. Not possible because of low margin requirements.

D. Use by commercials as a tool for helping farmers.

8. Without the proper structure of a trade:

A. You will take small losses and large profits.

B. You will be forced to use a computer when placing your orders.

C. Traders will have to rely on tips for good trades.

D. You have nothing.

LESSON 2, DAY 2

Setup, Trigger, and Follow-through: The Basics

INTRODUCTION

The market structure presented in Lesson 1 will be explained in greater detail in this lesson. Specific examples of *setup*, *trigger*, and *follow-through* (*S*, *T*, and *F*, respectively) will be given. In reading the material in this lesson, do not forget that the most important part of any trade is the structure. If you stray from the structure, you decrease your odds of success, increase your odds of making a mistake, and increase your odds of an emotional response. None of these are acceptable and they are inconsistent with profitable trading.

COMMON SETUPS

Many traders confuse setups with triggers. A *setup* is an indication that a given market is developing a pattern that could or should lead to action. While there are many patterns in the markets, there are only a handful that are reliable. The sad fact is that most traders follow patterns that are *not* reliable. Ask yourself the following questions about the methods you are currently using:

- How often has the pattern or method you are using been correct?
- Is the pattern completely objective and specific, or does it require you to make a judgment call?

- Does the pattern have specific entry and exit rules?
- Does the pattern or method give you an idea of risk and/or reward?

If your answer to any one of these is no, then I respectfully submit that you are either losing money with the pattern or if you *are* making money with it your luck will not last.

The performance statistics of some commonly used trading tools might interest and disappoint you. For example, the *daily reversal signal* is one of the most widely followed price patterns and it comes in two forms—up and down—defined as follows:

- *Daily reversal up.* The market drops below the previous daily low and closes above the previous daily close as shown in the simple example in Figure 2.1.
- *Daily reversal down.* The market goes above the previous daily high and closes below the previous daily close as shown in the simple example in Figure 2.2.

I programmed these two patterns on the computer for the S&P 500 futures. The computer examined all the instances of these two patterns from 1982 to 2004 and then I asked the following question:

How often after this pattern could a profit have been achieved the next day if a position was taken on the close of trading on the day of the reversal?

Figure 2.3 shows the results.

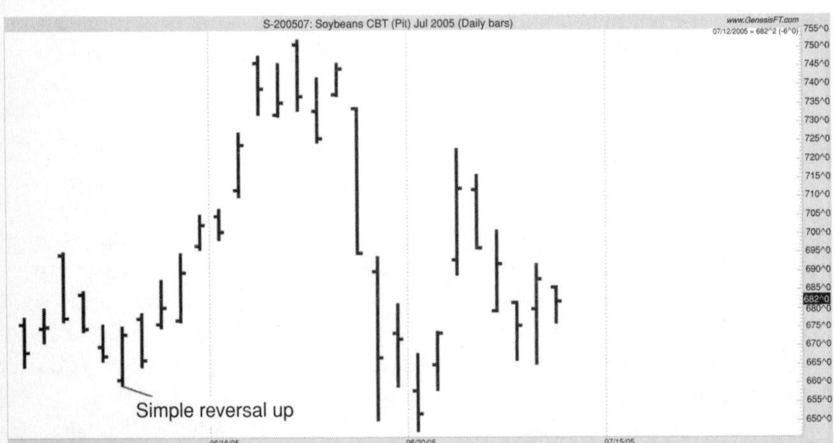

FIGURE 2.1 Simple reversal up.
Source: Courtesy of www.GenesisFT.com.

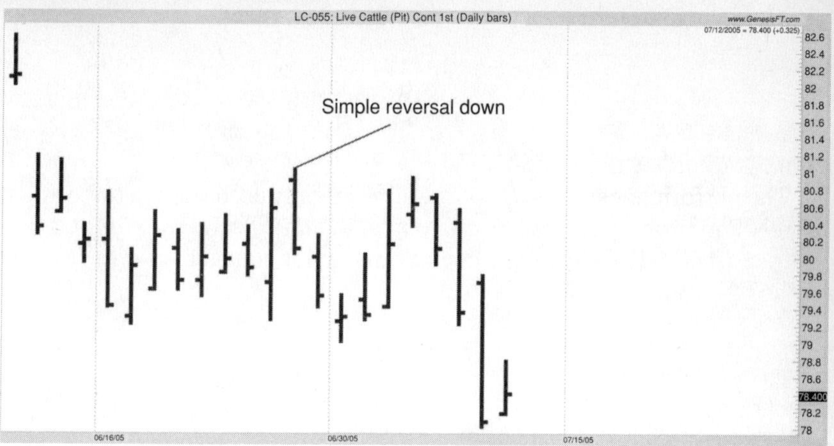

FIGURE 2.2 Simple reversal down.
Source: Courtesy of www.GenesisFT.com.

Overall			
Total Net Profit:	$39,250	Profit Factor ($Wins/$Losses):	**1.07**
Total Trades:	589	Winning Percentage:	**75.9%**
Average Trade:	$67	Payout Ratio (Avg Win/Loss):	**0.34**
Avg #of Bars in Trade:	3,93	Z-Score (W/L Predictability):	–4.9
Avg #of Trades per Year:	25.4	Percent in the Market:	39.5%
Max Closed-out Drawdown:	–$91,325	Max Intraday Drawdown:	–$91,350
Account Size Required:	$108,668	Return Pct:	36.1%
Open Equity:	$0	Kelly Ratio:	0.0515
Current Streak:	1 Losses	Optimal f:	0.13
Winning Trades		**Losing Trades**	
Total Winners:	447	Total Losers:	142
Gross Profit:	$578,200	Gross Loss:	–$538,950
Average Win:	$1,294	Average Loss:	–$3,795
Largest Win:	$14,675	Largest Loss:	–$15,025
Largest Drawdown in Win:	–$3,375	Largest Peak in Loss:	$10,788
Avg Drawdown in Win:	–$863	Avg Peak in Loss:	$508
Avg Run Up in Win:	$1,740	Avg Run Up in Loss:	$508
Avg Run Down in Win:	–$863	Avg Run Down in Loss:	–$3,795
Most Consec Wins:	50	Most Consec Losses:	5
Avg # of Consec Wins:	5.20	Avg # of Consec Losses:	1.63
Avg # of Bars in Wins:	3.66	Avg # of Bars in Losses:	4.77

FIGURE 2.3 Results of a simple reversal-up buy strategy.

Overall			
Total Net Profit:	–$15,175	Profit Factor ($Wins/$Losses):	**0.97**
Total Trades:	550	Winning Percentage:	**70.0%**
Average Trade:	$28	Payout Ratio (Avg Win/Loss):	**0.42**
Avg #of Bars in Trade:	4.75	Z-Score (W/L Predictability):	–1.1
Avg #of Trades per Year:	23.7	Percent in the Market:	44.6%
Max Closed-out Drawdown:	–$97,875	Max Intraday Drawdown:	–$97,900
Account Size Required:	$115,218	Return Pct:	–13.2%
Open Equity:	$0	Kelly Ratio:	–0.0182
Current Streak:	1 Wins	Optimal f:	–0.02
Winning Trades		**Losing Trades**	
Total Winners:	385	Total Losers:	165
Gross Profit:	$582,775	Gross Loss:	–$597,950
Average Win:	$1,514	Average Loss:	–$3,624
Largest Win:	$21,225	Largest Loss:	–$6,700
Largest Drawdown in Win:	–$3,438	Largest Peak in Loss:	$8,725
Avg Drawdown in Win:	–$949	Avg Peak in Loss:	$555
Avg Run Up in Win:	$2,242	Avg Run Up in Loss:	$555
Avg Run Down in Win:	–$949	Avg Run Down in Loss:	–$3,624
Most Consec Wins:	28	Most Consec Losses:	6
Avg # of Consec Wins:	3.47	Avg # of Consec Losses:	1.50
Avg # of Bars in Wins:	4.11	Avg # of Bars in Losses:	6.26

FIGURE 2.4 Results of a simple reversal-down sell strategy.

Look closely at the results and don't let yourself get fooled by the 75.9 percent winning trades. As you can see, the average trade made $67 after deducting $25 for slippage and commission. Note also that this method would have resulted in over $91,000 in draw down*, enough to wipe out most traders accounts. At best this is a marginal system. This record represented only the buy reversals.

The sell reversal historical record is shown in Figure 2.4.

The other statistics contained in Figures 2.2 through 2.4 are not relevant to this course*

As you can see, this approach revealed a 70 percent accuracy; but the profits were abysmal. Never ask what the percentage accuracy of a trading method is. This statistic is meaningless without knowledge of whether the method is profitable! In spite of the poor performance, the accuracy is impressive and there must be a way to take advantage of the pattern. There is a way, and that way is simple. All we need to do is to *add a trigger* to the method.

*Draw down: The maximum dollar amount of successive losses.

ADDING A TRIGGER

What if we added a trigger to each of these patterns? Would that perhaps make them more accurate and profitable? I took the simple reversal patterns and added one more variable as a trigger.

Buy Reversal

The buy-reversal pattern can be expressed as low of day 2 is lower than low of day 1; close of day 2 is higher than close of day 1 *and* close of day 3 is lower than the low of day 2, then *buy* on the close of day 3 and take profit on first profitable opening. You can see from the chart shown in Figure 2.5 that this pattern is counterintuitive. In other words, it is *not* what you would expect to see as a buy signal. It "looks like" it should be a sell rather than a buy. One of the key things I want to impress upon you is that you must think differently than most traders. *You must rid yourself of common thinking unless you want common results!*

Table 2.1 shows the historical performance of this pattern.

Do you see a significant difference? Which pattern would you rather trade?

Sell Reversal

The sell-reversal pattern can be expressed as high of day 2 is higher than high of day 1; close of day 2 is lower than close of day 1 and close of day 3

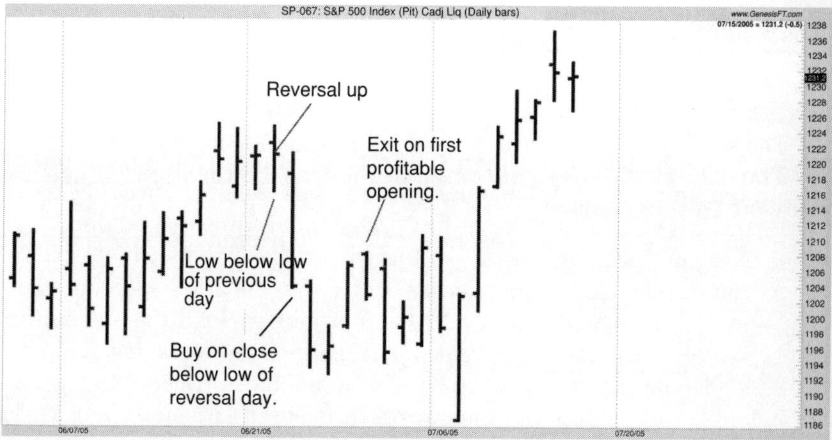

FIGURE 2.5 Reversal Pattern with Trigger.
Source: Courtesy of www.GenesisFT.com.

TABLE 2.1 Results of Buy Reversal with Trigger Summary—Long Trades Report

Name: Jake's Reversal Trades New
Symbol: SP-067

Overall			
Total Net Profit:	$79,513	Profit Factor ($Wins/$Losses):	2.50
Total Trades:	101	Winning Percentage:	91.1%
Average Trade:	$787	Payout Ratio (Avg. Win/Loss):	0.25
Avg. No. of Bars in Trade:	5.13	Z-Score (W/L Predictability):	0.1
Avg. No. of Trades per Year:	4.4	Percent in the Market:	8.8%
Max Closed-out Drawdown:	−$16,075	Max. Intraday Drawdown:	−$18,275
Account Size Required:	$35,593	Return Percentage:	223.4%
Open Equity:	$0	Kelly Ratio:	0.5472
Current Streak:	7 Wins	Optimal f:	0.61
Winning Trades		**Losing Trades**	
Total Winners:	92	Total Losers:	9
Gross Profit:	$132,363	Gross Loss:	−$52,850
Average Win:	$1,439	Average Loss:	−$5,872
Largest Win:	$9,900	Largest Loss:	−$7,400
Largest Drawdown in Win:	−$5,600	Largest Peak in Loss:	$2,175
Avg. Drawdown in Win:	−$1,384	Avg. Peak in Loss:	$782
Avg. Run Up in Win:	$1,879	Avg. Run-up in Loss:	$782
Avg. Run Down in Win:	−$1,384	Avg. Run-down in Loss:	−$5,872
Most Consec Wins:	25	Most Consecutive Losses:	2
Avg. No. of Consec Wins:	10.22	Avg. No. of Consecutive Losses:	1.13
Avg. No. of Bars in Wins:	5.29	Avg. No. of Bars in Losses:	3.44

is higher than high of day 2, then *sell* on close of day 3 and take profit on first profitable opening. Again, note that this is not what you would expect.

But does it work as well as the buy pattern in the previous section? Take a look at the performance history of this pattern as shown in Table 2.2.

As you can see, the sell pattern has been correct nearly 90 percent of the time—but it fails to make money. Is that a problem? No! If the buy pattern works we will use it. Because the sell pattern does not work, we avoid it.

It is all about knowing what works by adding a trigger and follow-through to a basic setup. In other words, it is about knowing what works *before* you put money on it. Ask yourself some important questions. Do you

TABLE 2.2 Results of Reversal-down Pattern with Trigger Summary—Short Trades Report

Name: Jake's Reversal Trades New
Symbol: SP-067

Overall			
Total Net Profit:	$338	Profit Factor ($Wins/$Losses):	1.00
Total Trades:	115	Winning Percentage:	87.8%
Average Trade:	$3	Payout Ratio (Avg. Win/Loss):	0.14
Avg. No. of Bars in Trade:	9.41	Z-Score (W/L Predictability):	0.0
Avg. No. of Trades per Year:	5.0	Percent in the Market:	18.4%
Max. Closed-out Drawdown:	−$29,450	Max. Intraday Drawdown:	−$32,450
Account Size Required:	$49,768	Return Percentage:	0.7%
Open Equity:	$0	Kelly Ratio:	0.0026
Current Streak:	2 Wins	Optimal f:	0.00
Winning Trades		**Losing Trades**	
Total Winners:	101	Total Losers:	14
Gross Profit:	$114,488	Gross Loss:	−$114,150
Average Win:	$1,134	Average Loss:	−$8,154
Largest Win:	$11,000	Largest Loss:	−$8,950
Largest Drawdown in Win:	−$7,275	Largest Peak in Loss:	$1,850
Avg. Drawdown in Win:	−$1,300	Avg. Peak in Loss:	$497
Avg. Run-up in Win:	$1,535	Avg. Run-up in Loss:	$497
Avg. Run-down in Win:	−$1,300	Avg. Run-down in Loss:	−$8,154
Most Consecutive Wins:	35	Most Consecutive Losses:	2
Avg. No. of Consecutive Wins:	7.77	Avg. No. of Consecutive Losses:	1.17
Avg. No. of Bars in Wins:	7.57	Avg. No. of Bars in Losses:	22.64

use methods like the Elliott Wave, Gann, or Fibonacci? Do you know if they work?

ADDING A FOLLOW-THROUGH

Now let us take the first reversal pattern (the buy pattern) and add a few follow-through alternatives. In other words, we vary the stop-loss and the exit. The results shown in this section's tables use two different stop-losses

TABLE 2.3 Reversal-up Pattern with Trigger and $2,500 Stop-loss Summary—Long Trades Report

Name: Jake's Reversal Trades New $2,500 stop-loss Exit on First Profitable Opening
Symbol: SP-067

Overall			
Total Net Profit:	$38,138	Profit Factor ($Wins/$Losses):	1.55
Total Trades:	105	Winning Percentage:	74.3%
Average Trade:	$363	Payout Ratio (Avg Win/Loss):	0.54
Avg. No. of Bars in Trade:	3.77	Z-Score (W/L Predictability):	0.4
Avg. No. of Trades per Year:	4.5	Percent in the Market:	6.8%
Max. Closed-out Drawdown:	−$17,450	Max Intraday Drawdown:	−$17,475
Account Size Required:	$34,793	Return Percentage:	109.6%
Open Equity:	$0	Kelly Ratio:	0.2638
Current Streak:	1 Losses	Optimal f:	0.26
Winning Trades		**Losing Trades**	
Total Winners:	78	Total Losers:	27
Gross Profit:	$107,413	Gross Loss:	−$69,275
Average Win:	$1,377	Average Loss:	−$2,566
Largest Win:	$9,350	Largest Loss:	−$3,250
Largest Drawdown in Win:	−$2,338	Largest Peak in Loss:	$3,400
Avg. Drawdown in Win:	−$743	Avg. Peak in Loss:	$254
Avg. Run-up in Win:	$1,788	Avg. Run-up in Loss:	$254
Avg Run-down in Win:	−$743	Avg. Run-down in Loss:	−$2,566
Most Consecutive Wins:	17	Most Consective Losses:	4
Avg. No. of Consecutive Wins:	3.71	Avg. No. of Consecutive Losses:	1.29
Avg. No. of Bars in Wins:	4.01	Avg. No. of Bars in Losses:	3.07

and exit methods. As you can see, follow-through in the form of a stop-loss and exit method can make a big difference.

Using a stop-loss of $2,500 with exit on the first profitable opening makes the results much less impressive, as you can see in Table 2.3.

Now let's change the exit method and the stop-loss to exit on the third profitable CLOSE with a $4900 stop-loss. Table 2.4 shows the results. Note that these examples are not recommended as trading strategies. They are merely included as illustrations.

As you can see, follow-through (also know as exit strategy) can make a major difference.

TABLE 2.4 Another Variation on Follow-through Summary—Long Trades Report

Name: Jake's Reversal Trades New $4900 stop-loss with exit on 3rd profitable close
Symbol: SP-067

Overall			
Total Net Profit:	$94,113	Profit Factor ($Wins/$Losses):	2.27
Total Trades:	102	Winning Percentage:	85.3%
Average Trade:	$923	Payout Ratio (Avg. Win/Loss):	0.39
Avg. No. of Bars in Trade:	5.22	Z-Score (W/L Predictability):	−0.4
Avg. No. of Trades per Year:	4.4	Percent in the Market:	9.1%
Max. Closed-out Drawdown:	−$17,900	Max. Intraday Drawdown:	−$18,225
Account Size Required:	$35,543	Return Percentage:	−264.8%
Open Equity:	$0	Kelly Ratio:	0.4778
Current Streak:	3 Wins	Optimal f:	0.39
Winning Trades		**Losing Trades**	
Total Winners:	87	Total Losers:	15
Gross Profit:	$167,988	Gross Loss:	−$73,875
Average Win:	$1,931	Average Loss:	−$4,925
Largest Win:	$15,150	Largest Loss:	−$4,925
Largest Drawdown in Win:	−$4,850	Largest Peak in Loss:	$3,400
Avg. Drawdown in Win:	−$1,482	Avg. Peak in Loss:	$970
Avg. Run-up in Win:	$2,644	Avg. Run-up in Loss:	$970
Avg. Run-down in Win:	−$1,482	Avg. Run-down in Loss:	−$4,925
Most Consecutive Wins:	25	Most Consecutive Losses:	2
Avg. No. of Consecutive Wins:	6.69	Avg. No. of Consecutive Losses:	1.25
Avg. No. of Bars in Wins:	5.52	Avg. No. of Bars in Losses:	3.47

S-T-F: THE COMPLETE APPROACH

To trade profitably you need to use a complete approach. Here are the elements of that approach:

- Specific entry and exit rules.
- 100 percent objective follow-through.
- Statistical performance history.
- No interpretation needed.

- Independent of any fundamentals or analysis.
- Capable of being completely computerized and analyzed.

This gives you a complete package that, in my view, places you way ahead of the vast majority of traders.

REVIEW

In this lesson, you learned a specific example of how we move through the setup, trigger, and follow-through method using a simple pattern. While the pattern in and of itself is not profitable, adding a trigger improves its accuracy and adding a follow-through method further improves the potential profits.

Now that you have seen an example of how we can take some commonly (but incorrectly) used setups and turn them into profitable methods, you're ready to move onto the first of five methods you will learn in this course. Lesson 3 introduces you to the first of these methods: the seasonal setup. Once you know how to find and evaluate the seasonal setups, we look at seasonal triggers and follow-through methods.

LESSON 2 QUIZ

Instructions: Circle the correct answers.

1. Most patterns in the markets:

   A. Make money.

   B. Lose money.

   C. Are used for hedging.

   D. Are based on weather.

2. A reversal up pattern occurs when:

   A. Traders quit for the day because the market goes limit up.

   B. A winning trade becomes a losing trade because a trader has become too emotional.

   C. A losing trade is closed out at the stop-loss on a Tuesday.

   D. The low of day 2 is lower than the low of day 1 and the close of day 2 is higher than the close of day 1.

3. A reversal down pattern occurs when:

   A. The high of day 2 is higher than the high of day 1 and the close of day 2 is lower than the close of day 1.

   B. Traders quit for the day because the market goes limit down.

   C. A losing trade becomes a winning trade because a trader has developed a new trading method.

   D. A losing trade is closed out at the stop-loss on a Friday.

4. Common thinking in trading:

   A. Gets common results.

   B. Will help you be successful.

   C. Is a good method to use.

   D. Uses exponential moving averages to get good results.

5. It is best to think differently than most traders:

   A. Because most traders think the same way.

   B. Because different thinkers get better results.

   C. Because common thinking gets common results.

   D. All of the above.

6. Looking only at the percentage accuracy of a trading method:

   A. Is the correct thing to do.

   B. Is the method used by professional traders.

   C. Can help you discover excellent trading methods.

   D. None of the above.

7. Choose all that apply: The following are aspects of a total approach to trading:

   A. Specific entry and exit rules.

   B. 100 percent objective follow-through.

   C. Statistical performance history.

   D. No interpretation needed.

8. Proper structure of every trade consists of:

   A. Having the right newsletter(s).

   B. Discussing every trade with your broker before you enter.

   C. Using the right systems.

   D. Setup, trigger, and follow-through.

LESSON 3, DAY 3

Seasonality and High-Odds Seasonal Setups

INTRODUCTION

One of the most enduring and reliable patterns in the markets is seasonality. While some people believe that seasonality is a function of weather or the seasons, this is not entirely true. Seasonality is the tendency for markets to move in certain directions during certain times of the year. These moves are caused by factors such as weather, harvest, planting, inventory buildup, holiday closing of mines, buying of building supplies prior to the building season, quarterly mutual fund portfolio adjustment, summer demand for meat, holiday demand for pork and poultry, summer unemployment increases, and a host of other variables. The reason or reasons for a seasonal move can be obvious—or they may not. While some traders care about the "why" of market moves, I do not. I am only interested in the fact that many moves are predictable to varying degrees of accuracy. Seasonals are found in virtually all data including commodities and stocks.

"Mine is not to reason why . . . mine is but to sell and buy." It makes no difference to me what causes markets to move as long as I can find reliable setups with a solid history of predictability. I suggest that you do the same. Note that I am not opposed to the use of fundamentals (i.e., the study of economic conditions that cause moves). I believe, however, that setups and timing are more important and that we do not need to know the causes of moves if our setups and triggers are valid.

TYPES OF SEASONALS

There are five basic types of seasonals:

1. *Monthly seasonal patterns in the cash markets.* These patterns give us a big picture idea of what has happened in the markets over a long period of time.
2. *Weekly seasonal patterns in commodities, stocks, and cash markets.* These give us a shorter term, week-to-week idea of price changes.
3. *Daily seasonal futures patterns.* These tell us the exact starting and ending dates of moves in stocks and futures.
4. *Preholiday seasonals patterns.* These patterns tend to occur with a high probability prior to major holidays.
5. *Seasonal patterns in spread and ratio relationships.* These patterns show how different months and/or markets have moved relative to each other.

The information derived from each of the above seasonal patterns gives us different information. My goal is to direct you to the most profitable and consistent of these patterns.

SEASONALS ARE SETUPS

As noted in Lesson 1, seasonals are setups that must be triggered. In Lesson 1, I cited a crude oil seasonal setup that had an exceptionally high probability of repetition. I have found over 1 million seasonal setups with accuracies from 75 percent to 100 percent. This does not mean that they are the perfect way to trade or that they will always work. We need a trigger and a follow-through method.

The seasonals I recommend that you use are *key date seasonals*. These seasonal setups provide the following information:

- The commodity and contract month, or the stock trade
- Whether to buy or sell
- The percentage historical accuracy
- The stop-loss in % of entry price (close only stop)
- The average profit per trade
- The average loss per trade
- The yearly profit or loss
- The cumulative profit or loss
- The profit/loss ratio

Having information places you above 95 percent of other traders in terms of their knowledge. Best of all, the information is purely objective and not a theory or a matter of opinion. It is a matter of fact based on history. There is no interpretation.

It is my opinion that interpretation in trading will open the door to subjective opinions, which will only increase your losses!

FINDING KEY DATE SEASONALS

There are several ways to find key date seasonals. You can write your own seasonal search program and find them or you can use my seasonal Web site, High Odds Seasonal Trades (HOST) at http://www.seasonaltrader.com/, where I have done all of the hard work for you. As part of this course, I will give you free access to this location for one month and show you how to use it. This information appears below. First, however, in the following tables, are examples of seasonals based on specific search criteria. These criteria are as follows:

- Setups that have been correct 75 percent of the time or more.
- Setups that have had a profit/loss ratio of 4 or higher. This means that in sum total the profits have been 4 times or more larger than the losses.
- Setups that last 25 calendar days or less since I believe that these are among the most reliable and consistent.

Using these criteria, I selected the setups for July shown in Table 3.1. Due to limitations of space, I have not included all of the setups.

This seasonal setup shows the historical record of buying Jly Hogs on the close of trading July 2 and exiting July 6 with a 1 percent stop-loss close only, over a period of 35 years. As you can see, the performance was impressive, with over 77 percent accuracy. But remember that this is only a seasonal setup. A trigger is required. The seasonal trigger will be discussed in Lesson 4.

The seasonal setup in Table 3.2 shows the historical record of buying Sep Heating Oil on the close of trading 7/25 and exiting on the close of trading 8/13 with a 4 percent stop-loss close only over a period of 25 years.

The setup in Table 3.3 shows a sell seasonal in Sep Soybeans from the entry date of 7/14 to the exit date of 7/30 with a 5 percent stop-loss close only over a 36-year period. As you can see, the accuracy has been over 77 percent with a large average profit per trade.

This setup shows a short sell seasonal in the Sep Canadian Dollar over the last 28 years from 7/17 to 7/24 with a 1 percent stop-loss close only. The record here is also impressive with over 82 percent accuracy.

TABLE 3.1 The High-Odds Seasonal Trade in July Hog Futures

Long Jly Lean Hogs		**Enter: 7/2**	**Exit: 7/6**	**Stop %: 1.00**	**P/L Ratio: 11.1**	**Trade #119061106**
Contract Year	**Date In**	**Price In**	**Date Out**	**Price Out**	**Profit/Loss**	**Total**
1970	2-Jul	26.35	6-Jul	26.4	0.05	0.05
1971	2-Jul	21.75	6-Jul	21.75	0	0.05
1972	3-Jul	30.4	6-Jul	30.22	−0.18	−0.13
1973	2-Jul	43.47	6-Jul	43.6	0.13	0
1974	2-Jul	36.95	8-Jul	38.97	2.02	2.02
1975	2-Jul	53.67	7-Jul	55.7	2.03	4.05
1976	2-Jul	50.05	6-Jul	49.02	−1.03	3.02
1977	5-Jul	48.12	6-Jul	48.57	0.45	3.47
1978	3-Jul	47.27	6-Jul	48.17	0.9	4.37
1979	2-Jul	40.2	6-Jul	41.37	1.17	5.54
1980	2-Jul	42.75	7-Jul	42.5	−0.25	5.29
1981	2-Jul	53.47	6-Jul	53.95	0.48	5.77
1982	2-Jul	60.02	6-Jul	60.12	0.1	5.87
1983	5-Jul	45.77	6-Jul	46.22	0.45	6.32
1984	2-Jul	54.7	6-Jul	55.12	0.42	6.74
1985	2-Jul	49.67	8-Jul	49.97	0.3	7.04
1986	2-Jul	59.67	7-Jul	61.55	1.88	8.92
1987	2-Jul	60.1	6-Jul	60.57	0.47	9.39
1988	5-Jul	44.07	6-Jul	44.57	0.5	9.89
1989	3-Jul	47.17	6-Jul	46.77	−0.4	9.49
1990	2-Jul	61.27	6-Jul	61.6	0.33	9.82
1991	2-Jul	53.75	8-Jul	54.85	1.1	10.92
1992	2-Jul	46.72	6-Jul	46.65	−0.07	10.85
1993	2-Jul	49.27	6-Jul	49.12	−0.15	10.7
1994	5-Jul	44.62	6-Jul	44.8	0.18	10.88
1995	3-Jul	45.9	6-Jul	46.72	0.82	11.7
1996	2-Jul	57.32	8-Jul	59.65	2.33	14.03
1997	2-Jul	83.25	7-Jul	83.2	−0.05	13.98
1998	2-Jul	57.6	6-Jul	57.95	0.35	14.33
1999	2-Jul	41.75	6-Jul	42.57	0.82	15.15
2000	3-Jul	70.35	6-Jul	71.15	0.8	15.95
2001	2-Jul	73.55	6-Jul	74.55	1	16.95
2002	2-Jul	52.3	8-Jul	54.9	2.6	19.55
2003	2-Jul	64.15	7-Jul	65.85	1.7	21.25
2004	2-Jul	79.12	6-Jul	79.37	0.25	21.5
Trades:		Winners:	Losers:		% Winners:	Daily PF:
35		27	8		77.14	0.2187
Avg. Profit:		Avg. Loss:	% Avg. Profit:		% Avg. Loss:	Bottom of
0.8751		−0.2662	1.69		−0.57	Form

TABLE 3.2 The Seasonal Trade in September Heating Oil Futures

Long Sep Htg Oil		Enter: 7/25	Exit: 8/13	Stop %: 4.00	P/L Ratio: 6.2	Trade #11253528
Contract Year	**Date In**	**Price In**	**Date Out**	**Price Out**	**Profit/Loss**	**Total**
1980	25-Jul	0.782	8-Aug	0.75	−0.032	−0.032
1981	27-Jul	0.9471	13-Aug	0.9516	0.0045	−0.0275
1982	26-Jul	0.8701	13-Aug	0.8914	0.0213	−0.0062
1983	25-Jul	0.8302	15-Aug	0.861	0.0308	0.0246
1984	25-Jul	0.7377	13-Aug	0.7583	0.0206	0.0452
1985	25-Jul	0.7126	13-Aug	0.7354	0.0228	0.068
1986	25-Jul	0.3266	13-Aug	0.4225	0.0959	0.1639
1987	27-Jul	0.538	13-Aug	0.5417	0.0037	0.1676
1988	25-Jul	0.4467	4-Aug	0.4246	−0.0221	0.1455
1989	25-Jul	0.5001	14-Aug	0.5004	0.0003	0.1458
1990	25-Jul	0.5794	13-Aug	0.7505	0.1711	0.3169
1991	25-Jul	0.5945	13-Aug	0.5977	0.0032	0.3201
1992	27-Jul	0.6291	3-Aug	0.598	−0.0311	0.289
1993	26-Jul	0.5132	13-Aug	0.536	0.0228	0.3118
1994	25-Jul	0.5071	12-Aug	0.4857	−0.0214	0.2904
1995	25-Jul	0.4703	14-Aug	0.4877	0.0174	0.3078
1996	25-Jul	0.5642	13-Aug	0.6001	0.0359	0.3437
1997	25-Jul	0.5464	13-Aug	0.5604	0.014	0.3577
1998	27-Jul	0.376	3-Aug	0.3581	−0.0179	0.3398
1999	26-Jul	0.5192	13-Aug	0.5569	0.0377	0.3775
2000	25-Jul	0.7589	14-Aug	0.8734	0.1145	0.492
2001	25-Jul	0.7127	13-Aug	0.7419	0.0292	0.5212
2002	25-Jul	0.6837	13-Aug	0.6942	0.0105	0.5317
2003	25-Jul	0.7834	13-Aug	0.807	0.0236	0.5553
2004	26-Jul	1.1233	13-Aug	1.2145	0.0912	0.6465
Trades: 25		Winners: 20	Losers: 5		% Winners: 80	Daily PF: 0.002
Avg. Profit: 0.0385		Avg. Loss: −0.0249	% Avg. Profit: 6.44		% Avg. Loss: −4.59	Bottom of Form

S-T-F: APPLICATION

The next step I recommend is to evaluate each setup on the basis of five factors:

1. Accuracy 75 percent or higher.
2. P/L ratio 4 or higher.

TABLE 3.3 The Seasonal Trade in September Soybean Futures

Short Sep Soybeans		**Enter: 7/14**	**Exit: 7/30**	**Stop%: 5.00**	**P/L Ratio: 4.0**	**Trade #110339480**
Contract Year	**Date In**	**Price In**	**Date Out**	**Price Out**	**Profit/Loss**	**Total**
1969	14-Jul	246.5	30-Jul	246.75	−0.25	−0.25
1970	14-Jul	294.5	30-Jul	283.25	11.25	11
1971	14-Jul	342	30-Jul	330.13	11.88	22.88
1972	14-Jul	336.38	31-Jul	334.5	1.88	24.75
1973	16-Jul	760	17-Jul	800	−40	−15.25
1974	15-Jul	661.5	18-Jul	716.5	−55	−70.25
1975	14-Jul	550.25	25-Jul	592.25	−42	−112.25
1976	14-Jul	738	30-Jul	608.5	129.5	17.25
1977	14-Jul	626.5	1-Aug	547.5	79	96.25
1978	14-Jul	628.5	31-Jul	621.75	6.75	103
1979	16-Jul	763	30-Jul	711	52	155
1980	14-Jul	788.5	30-Jul	753.75	34.75	189.75
1981	14-Jul	750.75	30-Jul	729.5	21.25	211
1982	14-Jul	621.75	30-Jul	600.75	21	232
1983	14-Jul	643.75	19-Jul	676.75	−33	199
1984	16-Jul	661	30-Jul	609.5	51.5	250.5
1985	15-Jul	570.25	30-Jul	519.25	51	301.5
1986	14-Jul	491	16-Jul	516.75	−25.75	275.75
1987	14-Jul	528.25	30-Jul	523.5	4.75	280.5
1988	14-Jul	956.5	1-Aug	823.5	133	413.5
1989	14-Jul	669.5	31-Jul	588	81.5	495
1990	16-Jul	606.25	30-Jul	593.75	12.5	507.5
1991	15-Jul	528.75	23-Jul	562.5	−33.75	473.75
1992	14-Jul	573.25	30-Jul	560.75	12.5	486.25
1993	14-Jul	709.25	30-Jul	686.5	22.75	509
1994	14-Jul	590.25	1-Aug	571.5	18.75	527.75
1995	14-Jul	625	31-Jul	606	19	546.75
1996	15-Jul	822.25	30-Jul	744.75	77.5	624.25
1997	14-Jul	674	30-Jul	670	4	628.25
1998	14-Jul	596.25	30-Jul	575.25	21	649.25
1999	14-Jul	419.25	21-Jul	451.25	−32	617.25
2000	14-Jul	450.25	31-Jul	444.5	5.75	623
2001	16-Jul	509.75	30-Jul	504	5.75	628.75
2002	15-Jul	547.5	30-Jul	531.5	16	644.75
2003	14-Jul	555.5	30-Jul	526.75	28.75	673.5
2004	14-Jul	681.5	30-Jul	574.5	107	780.5
Trades: 36		Winners: 28	Losers: 8		% Winners: 77.78	Daily PF: 2.3264
Avg. Profit: 37.2232		Avg. Loss: −32.7187	% Avg. Profit: 5.48		% Avg. Loss: −5.71	Bottom of Form

TABLE 3.4 The Seasonal Trade in September Canadian Dollar Futures

Short Sep Canada $		**Enter: 7/17**	**Exit: 7/24**	**Stop %: 1.00**	**P/LRatio: 5.6**	**Trade #107869168**
Contract Year	**Date In**	**Price In**	**Date Out**	**Price Out**	**Profit/Loss**	**Total**
1977	18-Jul	0.942	25-Jul	0.9399	0.0021	0.0021
1978	17-Jul	0.8903	24-Jul	0.8899	0.0004	0.0025
1979	17-Jul	0.8598	24-Jul	0.857	0.0028	0.0053
1980	17-Jul	0.8665	24-Jul	0.8642	0.0023	0.0076
1981	17-Jul	0.8283	24-Jul	0.8195	0.0088	0.0164
1982	19-Jul	0.7921	26-Jul	0.7875	0.0046	0.021
1983	18-Jul	0.812	25-Jul	0.8116	0.0004	0.0214
1984	17-Jul	0.7509	24-Jul	0.7575	−0.0066	0.0148
1985	17-Jul	0.7399	24-Jul	0.7383	0.0016	0.0164
1986	17-Jul	0.7251	24-Jul	0.7177	0.0074	0.0238
1987	17-Jul	0.7564	24-Jul	0.7455	0.0109	0.0347
1988	18-Jul	0.8266	25-Jul	0.8191	0.0075	0.0422
1989	17-Jul	0.8352	24-Jul	0.837	−0.0018	0.0404
1990	17-Jul	0.8587	24-Jul	0.8578	0.0009	0.0413
1991	17-Jul	0.8672	24-Jul	0.8637	0.0035	0.0448
1992	17-Jul	0.838	24-Jul	0.8367	0.0013	0.0461
1993	19-Jul	0.7808	26-Jul	0.7802	0.0006	0.0467
1994	18-Jul	0.7247	25-Jul	0.7242	0.0005	0.0472
1995	17-Jul	0.7371	24-Jul	0.7364	0.0007	0.0479
1996	17-Jul	0.7291	24-Jul	0.7301	−0.001	0.0469
1997	17-Jul	0.7284	24-Jul	0.726	0.0024	0.0493
1998	17-Jul	0.6723	24-Jul	0.6677	0.0046	0.0539
1999	19-Jul	0.6717	26-Jul	0.6629	0.0088	0.0627
2000	17-Jul	0.6761	24-Jul	0.6838	−0.0077	0.055
2001	17-Jul	0.6487	24-Jul	0.6489	−0.0002	0.0548
2002	17-Jul	0.6475	24-Jul	0.6354	0.0121	0.0669
2003	17-Jul	0.7141	24-Jul	0.7134	0.0007	0.0676
2004	19-Jul	0.7634	26-Jul	0.7507	0.0127	0.0803
Trades:		Winners:	Losers:		% Winners:	Daily PF:
28		23	5		82.14	0.0006
Avg Prof:		Avg Loss:	% Avg Prof:		% Avg Loss:	Bottom of
0.0042		−0.0034	0.56		−0.47	Form

3. No more than two consecutive losses as shown in the Profit/Loss Ratio columns in Tables 3.1 through 3.4).
4. Average profit of $400 or more as shown in the cell of each table that is labeled Avg. Profit. This is the average profit in points. It must be converted to dollars using the appropriate tick value for the given market.

5. A positive growth trend. This is the figure that appears in the Cumulative Profit column of each table. We want the most recent cumulative profit, in this case for the year 2004 to be higher than it was 10 years ago.

Any setup that passes 4 of these 5 tests is kept as a valid setup and the next step, the trigger, is applied. This step will be discussed in Lesson 4.

LOGGING INTO WWW.SEASONALTRADER.COM

You can find setups like these yourself by going to www.seasonaltrader.com, where you can sign up for a free trial (follow the links to sign up for the free trial to HOST Online). Once you're logged in, visit the FAQs page and read the simple *Quick Start Guide*.

You are now ready to practice finding trades with the rules that I gave you. Practice and get ready for Lesson 4: The Seasonal Trigger and Follow-through.

REVIEW

In this lesson, I showed you how to find seasonal setups with the highest odds of success. You learned the correct filters for these setups and you were given some examples of trades and their historical records. You were given instructions on how to log into the High Odds Seasonal Trades Web site along with your password and login name.

After you have practiced finding seasonal setups at the HOST Web site, you will be ready to learn the seasonal triggers and follow-through methods. The key to effective application of this method is practice and a thorough understanding and application of the rules. Lesson 4 teaches you the trigger and follow-through methods for this approach.

LESSON 3 QUIZ

Instructions: Circle the correct answers.

1. Seasonal trade patterns are based on weather:

   A. Correct.

   B. Incorrect.

C. In some cases.

D. Only when the weather destroys crops.

2. Seasonality:

A. Is the "holy grail" of futures and stock trading.

B. Is used by farmers when they market their crops.

C. Can only be used in conjunction with government crop reports.

D. Is only one part of a complete approach to trading.

3. There are several types of seasonal trade setups:

A. True only in commodities.

B. True only in stocks.

C. Always true.

D. Never true.

4. Preholiday seasonal patterns (select all that apply):

A. Are patterns that occur on the day prior to major holidays.

B. Are caused by traders going on vacations.

C. Are triggers.

D. Are a form of seasonality.

5. A key date seasonal setup (select all that apply):

A. Tells you the exact entry and exit date for a trade.

B. Gives you a specific stop-loss.

C. Is based on a vast amount of historical data

D. Is the first step in a total approach using setup, trigger, and follow-through.

6. Interpretation of trading indicators:

A. Is the correct thing to do at all times.

B. Is best used for day trading.

C. Can help you develop excellent trading strategies.

D. Will often open the door to subjective opinions thereby increasing losses.

7. Choose all that apply:

A. Seasonality is a follow-through method.

B. Weekly seasonals are only used by hedge fund managers.

C. Stocks and futures have seasonal patterns.

D. No interpretation is needed with seasonals.

8. Seasonal patterns can be found in:

A. Stocks.

B. Futures.

C. Spreads.

D. All of the above.

LESSON 4, DAY 4

The Seasonal Trigger

INTRODUCTION

As you know from Lessons 1 through 3, a trigger is necessary even if we have a highly reliable setup. In the previous lesson, I showed how to find valid setups and how to filter them using five criteria. Now comes the next step in the process—the trigger.

For my work, a trigger is what most other traders call a "timing signal." Based on my extensive research and experience, I believe that if you combine a valid setup with an effective trigger, then a winning combination is the result. Just as a carpenter or mechanic must select the right tool for the right job, a trader must select the right trigger for a setup. A hammer cannot do a job that calls for a wrench. Lest I continue to overstate the obvious, my message should be clear. I have found that the preferred trigger for my seasonals is the *stochastic indicator* (SI). However, I do not use the SI in the way that most traders do.

STOCHASTIC K 14 AND 5

Using the SI as a trigger with seasonal setups involves the following rules of application:

- Use a 14-period slow stochastic %K with 5-bar smoothing—and do not use %D. The stochastic %K configuration should be readily available

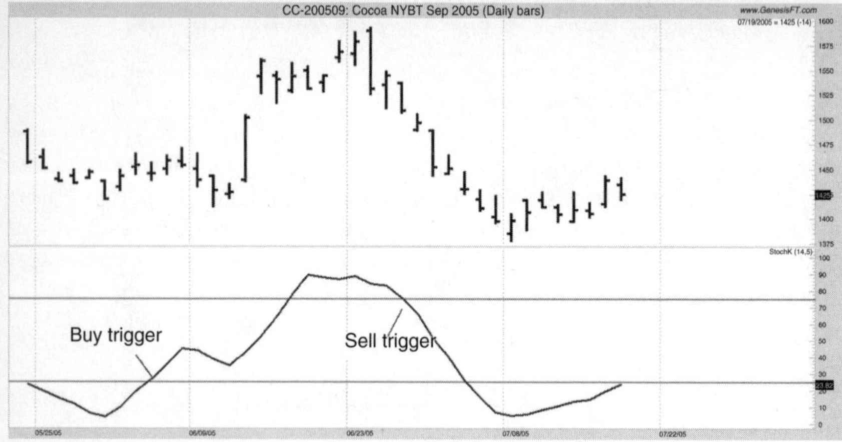

FIGURE 4.1 The buy and sell triggers for seasonal setups.
Source: Courtesy of www.GenesisFT.com.

on most quality charting programs. I use, for example, the Genesis Navigator™ program (www.genesisft.com).

- A buy trigger occurs when SI %K has been below 25 percent and has gone back above it.
- A sell trigger occurs when SI %K has been above 75 percent and has gone back below it.

See Figure 4.1 for a visual representation of these two conditions.
Here is the procedure:

1. Once you have selected your seasonal setups, and evaluated the five factors, arrange them in date order. At the end of the trading day, before the entry date for your setup, examine the stochastic to see if there has been a trigger. If the trigger is consistent with the setup and it is clear that the trigger will be maintained, then enter the order to be executed on the close of trading (MOC order).
2. If it is not clear (i.e., the SI reading is close to the required value), then do not enter the order but wait until the closing price is available and then make your decision. If there has been a trigger, then enter on the opening of the next day.
3. Every trade has a stop-loss as it appears on the top of the seasonal historical listing. All stops are close only.*

*Not all exchanges accept "close-only" orders. In such cases use the next day opening for entry or exit.

4. More details about the stop-loss and follow-up are given in the next lesson on follow-through.
5. If a trade does not trigger on the exact entry date, then you can allow 15 percent more time as measured by the length of the trade. As an example, if a trade is to be entered on 6/1 and exited on 6/15, then the length of the trade is 14 days. If it does not trigger on the entry date, or on the close of trading the next business day, then allow the trade 15 percent more time. In this case it would be 15 percent of 14 days, which is 2.1 days. Round all fractions up to the next highest full day or, in this case, three days. These are trading days.

AN EXAMPLE

I took two of the seasonal setups from Lesson 3 to use as examples of the seasonal trigger procedure here. The lean hog trade is shown in Table 4.1.

This seasonal setup shows the historical record of buying Jly Hogs on the close of trading July 2 and exiting July 6 with a 1 percent stop-loss close only, over a period of 35 years. As you can see, the performance was impressive. The trade met all but one of our five required factors. The ideal entry date was 7/2. The market was closed on 7/2/05 and also on 7/3/05 and 7/4/05. Accordingly, the trade was entered on the close of trading 7/5/05 and exited on the close of trading 7/6/05.

The SI timing chart (Figure 4.2) contains notes on the trigger. This exit was without the follow-through method, which will be discussed in Lesson 5.

Now let's look at a sell setup and trigger. The seasonal setup Table 4.2 was also shown in the last lesson.

This setup shows a short sell seasonal in the Sep Canadian Dollar over the last 28 years from 7/17 to 7/24 with a 1 percent stop-loss close only. The record here is also impressive with over 82 percent accuracy. This trade met all five of our filter criteria. Figure 4.3 shows the chart as of the close of trading on 7/18/05 along with my notations.

This trade has triggered. The outcome is to be decided since the trade is only now being entered as the present lesson is being written.

REVIEW

In this lesson, you learned how seasonal setups with the highest odds of success are triggered using the SI. You learned the correct triggers for these setups and you were given some examples of trades and their application.

TABLE 4.1 The Seasonal Trade in July Hogs with the Timing Trigger as Noted Earlier

Jul Lean Hogs Long		Enter: 7/2	Exit: 7/6	Stop %: 1.00	P/L Ratio: 11.1	Trade #119061106
Contract Year	**Date In**	**Price In**	**Date Out**	**Price Out**	**Profit/Loss**	**Total**
1970	7/2	26.35	7/6	26.40	0.05	0.05
1971	7/2	21.75	7/6	21.75	0.00	0.05
1972	7/3	30.40	7/6	30.22	−0.18	−0.13
1973	7/2	43.47	7/6	43.60	0.13	0.00
1974	7/2	36.95	7/8	38.97	2.02	2.02
1975	7/2	53.67	7/7	55.70	2.03	4.05
1976	7/2	50.05	7/6	49.02	−1.03	3.02
1977	7/5	48.12	7/6	48.57	0.45	3.47
1978	7/3	47.27	7/6	48.17	0.90	4.37
1979	7/2	40.20	7/6	41.37	1.17	5.54
1980	7/2	42.75	7/7	42.50	−0.25	5.29
1981	7/2	53.47	7/6	53.95	0.48	5.77
1982	7/2	60.02	7/6	60.12	0.10	5.87
1983	7/5	45.77	7/6	46.22	0.45	6.32
1984	7/2	54.70	7/6	55.12	0.42	6.74
1985	7/2	49.67	7/8	49.97	0.30	7.04
1986	7/2	59.67	7/7	61.55	1.88	8.92
1987	7/2	60.10	7/6	60.57	0.47	9.39
1988	7/5	44.07	7/6	44.57	0.50	9.89
1989	7/3	47.17	7/6	46.77	−0.40	9.49
1990	7/2	61.27	7/6	61.60	0.33	9.82
1991	7/2	53.75	7/8	54.85	1.10	10.92
1992	7/2	46.72	7/6	46.65	−0.07	10.85
1993	7/2	49.27	7/6	49.12	−0.15	10.70
1994	7/5	44.62	7/6	44.80	0.18	10.88
1995	7/3	45.90	7/6	46.72	0.82	11.70
1996	7/2	57.32	7/8	59.65	2.33	14.03
1997	7/2	83.25	7/7	83.20	−0.05	13.98
1998	7/2	57.60	7/6	57.95	0.35	14.33
1999	7/2	41.75	7/6	42.57	0.82	15.15
2000	7/3	70.35	7/6	71.15	0.80	15.95
2001	7/2	73.55	7/6	74.55	1.00	16.95
2002	7/2	52.30	7/8	54.90	2.60	19.55
2003	7/2	64.15	7/7	65.85	1.70	21.25
2004	7/2	79.12	7/6	79.37	0.25	21.50
Trades: 35		Winners: 27	Losers: 8		% Winners: 77.14	Daily PF: 0.2187
Avg. Profit: 0.8751		Avg Loss: 0.2662	% Avg. Prof: 1.69		% Avg. Loss: −0.57	

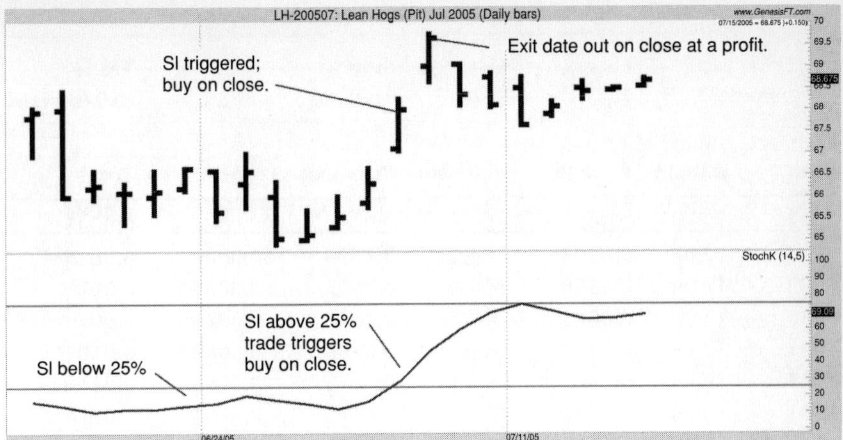

FIGURE 4.2 Notes on the trigger.
Source: Courtesy of www.GenesisFT.com.

Now that you have learned to find the seasonal setups at the H.O.S.T. Web site, and now that you know how to apply the seasonal triggers, you will want to practice. The next chapter describes three follow-through methods—which one you use depends on how aggressive you want to be. The key to effective application of this method is practice and a thorough understanding and application of the rules as discussed. Lesson 5 completes the setup, trigger and follow-through for method #1, seasonality.

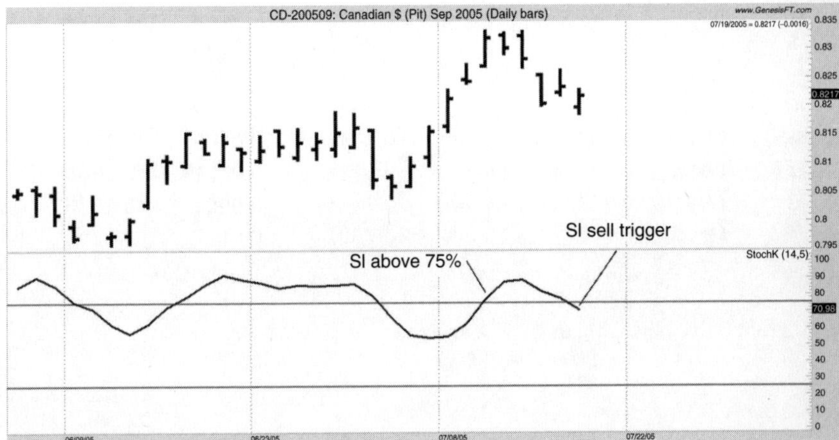

FIGURE 4.3 The seasonal trigger using stochastic 14 and 5 as discussed earlier.
Source: Courtesy of www.GenesisFT.com.

TABLE 4.2 Canadian Dollar Seasonal Trade with the Trigger

	Short Sep Canada $	**Enter: 7/17**	**Exit: 7/24**	**Stop %: 1.00**	**P/L Ratio: 5.6**	**Trade #107869168**
Contract Year	**Date In**	**Price In**	**Date Out**	**Price Out**	**Profit/Loss**	**Total**
1977	18-Jul	0.942	25-Jul	0.9399	0.0021	0.0021
1978	17-Jul	0.8903	24-Jul	0.8899	0.0004	0.0025
1979	17-Jul	0.8598	24-Jul	0.857	0.0028	0.0053
1980	17-Jul	0.8665	24-Jul	0.8642	0.0023	0.0076
1981	17-Jul	0.8283	24-Jul	0.8195	0.0088	0.0164
1982	19-Jul	0.7921	26-Jul	0.7875	0.0046	0.021
1983	18-Jul	0.812	25-Jul	0.8116	0.0004	0.0214
1984	17-Jul	0.7509	24-Jul	0.7575	−0.0066	0.0148
1985	17-Jul	0.7399	24-Jul	0.7383	0.0016	0.0164
1986	17-Jul	0.7251	24-Jul	0.7177	0.0074	0.0238
1987	17-Jul	0.7564	24-Jul	0.7455	0.0109	0.0347
1988	18-Jul	0.8266	25-Jul	0.8191	0.0075	0.0422
1989	17-Jul	0.8352	24-Jul	0.837	−0.0018	0.0404
1990	17-Jul	0.8587	24-Jul	0.8578	0.0009	0.0413
1991	17-Jul	0.8672	24-Jul	0.8637	0.0035	0.0448
1992	17-Jul	0.838	24-Jul	0.8367	0.0013	0.0461
1993	19-Jul	0.7808	26-Jul	0.7802	0.0006	0.0467
1994	18-Jul	0.7247	25-Jul	0.7242	0.0005	0.0472
1995	17-Jul	0.7371	24-Jul	0.7364	0.0007	0.0479
1996	17-Jul	0.7291	24-Jul	0.7301	−0.001	0.0469
1997	17-Jul	0.7284	24-Jul	0.726	0.0024	0.0493
1998	17-Jul	0.6723	24-Jul	0.6677	0.0046	0.0539
1999	19-Jul	0.6717	26-Jul	0.6629	0.0088	0.0627
2000	17-Jul	0.6761	24-Jul	0.6838	−0.0077	0.055
2001	17-Jul	0.6487	24-Jul	0.6489	−0.0002	0.0548
2002	17-Jul	0.6475	24-Jul	0.6354	0.0121	0.0669
2003	17-Jul	0.7141	24-Jul	0.7134	0.0007	0.0676
2004	19-Jul	0.7634	26-Jul	0.7507	0.0127	0.0803
Trades: 28		Winners: 23	Losers: 5		% Winners: 82.14	Daily PF: 0.0006
Avg. Profit: 0.0042		Avg. Loss: −0.0034	% Avg. Profit: 0.56		% Avg. Loss: −0.47	

LESSON 4 QUIZ

Instructions: Label the SI buy and sell triggers on the following charts.

1.

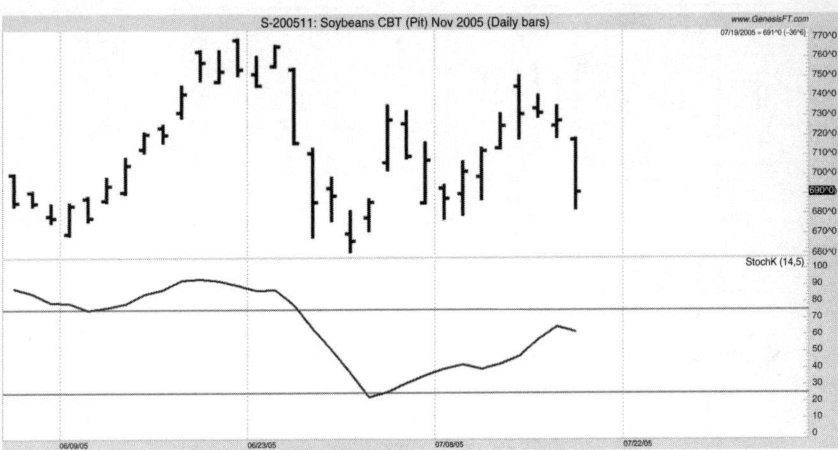

Source: Courtesy of www.GenesisFT.com.

2.

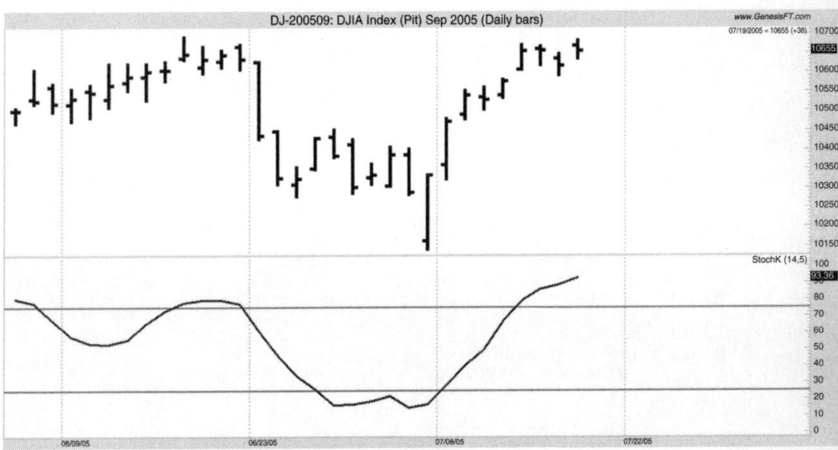

Source: Courtesy of www.GenesisFT.com.

3.

Source: Courtesy of www.GenesisFT.com.

4.

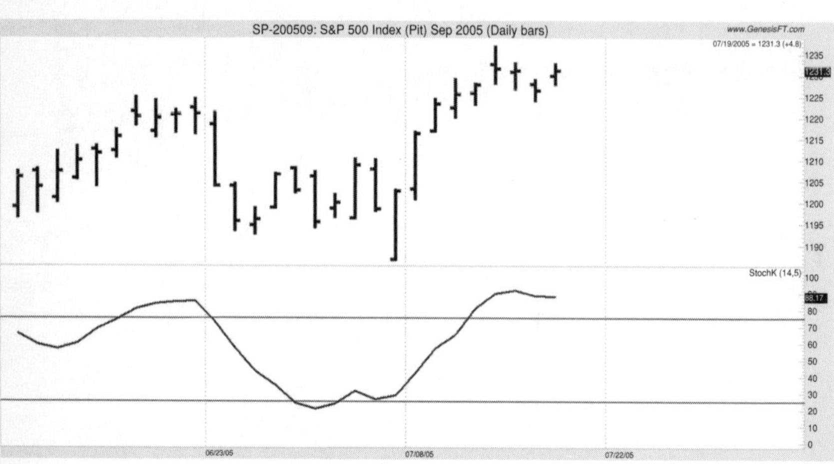

Source: Courtesy of www.GenesisFT.com.

5.

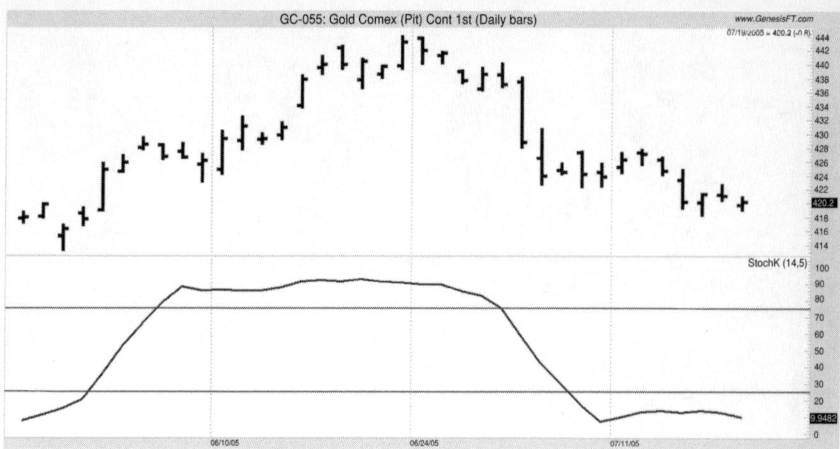

Source: Courtesy of www.GenesisFT.com.

LESSON 5, DAY 5

Follow-through

INTRODUCTION

An integral part of all trading is follow-through. As you will recall, follow-through is the third part of the STF method discussed in the first four lessons. For all too many traders, this is the weak link in the chain inasmuch as they are unable to manage risk. But managing risk, in the form of a stop-loss, is only part of the your success formula. Traders must also know how to maximize profits. In the absence of a profit maximizing strategy, you will not make money. In the absence of a profit maximizing strategy, your fate will be like that of most traders—you will make your broker rich, you may have fun trading. but in the long run you will not make money—in fact, you will lose money.

This lesson shows you my recommended profit-maximizing strategy for seasonal trading. The same approach, with some variations, is used in the other methods you learn in this course.

RISK MANAGEMENT USING A STOP-LOSS

The most common form of risk management is the stop-loss. There is much to be said for the use of stop-losses. They are, however, often used incorrectly and more often misunderstood. Most traders are misguided in their use of stops. Here are the common fallacies associated with stops:

- *If you use a small stop-loss with every trade your losses will be small.* The good news about this belief is that your individual losses will be small. The bad news is that you will lose almost every time because your stop-losses are too small to allow the markets room to make their normal random fluctuations.
- *A stop-loss should be based on how much you can afford to risk on a trade.* This is utter nonsense. The markets "don't give a hoot" about what you can afford to risk. Stops should be a function of the system or method you are using!
- *A stop-loss alone is not the key to profits.* A stop-loss is only part of the procedure.
- *Many traders like to use trailing stop-losses.* A trailing stop-loss is used to protect profits as a trade moves in the right direction. The problem with trailing stops is that they are often too close to the market. This results in trades being stopped out before the big profits are made.

TYPES OF STOP-LOSSES

For the methods I use and teach the following types of stop-losses will be employed:

- *Initial stop or money management stop (MMS).* The purpose of this stop is to limit your loss. Such stops are ideally based on the system or method being used as opposed to what you are able to risk. As noted earlier, what you are willing or able to risk is not a factor as far as the markets are concerned.
- *Break-even stop (BES).* Once a trade has achieved its initial profit target or floor level (FL), the stop-loss will be raised to breakeven. Breakeven is the price at which you entered. I do not consider commissions as part of the break-even calculation.
- *Trailing stop (TS).* This is a stop that is entered once a trade has reached its floor level.
- *Parabolic stop (PS).* This is a trailing stop based on the parabolic indicator. The PS is used only when a market has made a very large move in your favor.

SEASONAL TRADE STOP-LOSS AND FOLLOW-UP

As noted in previous lessons, every trade has a stop-loss. The stop-loss is an initial stop. In other words, the stop will change as part of the follow-through technique. All stops for the seasonal trades are shown at the top of the historical trade listing. The stops are close only. Once a seasonal trade has achieved its average profit per trade, as shown on the seasonal historical listing, the stop is moved to a break-even stop. On the exit date for the trade, it is closed out at the end of the day using a *market-on-close* (MOC) order if it has not already been stopped out at the break-even stop. Aggressive traders will want to stay in winning trades beyond the exit date as discussed later in this lesson.

THREE TYPES OF FOLLOW-THROUGH

I believe that traders should employ three types of follow-through on trades. How they do this depends on how aggressive or conservative they want to be in their trading. Generally, these methods apply to all of the methods you will learn in this course. The following sections outline the three types of follow-through, step by step, for the seasonal trades.

Trading in One Contract

Many traders can only trade one contract because they do not have much capital in their account. Without a doubt, the odds of success are considerably lower if you begin with a small amount of money. Traders who begin with a small amount of money (i.e., $5,000 or less) tend to have what I call a "profit-taking" mentality. They want to grab profits as quickly as they can since they believe that this will allow them to build up their account equity. In a perfect world, this would be the case, however, in reality this does not work. Why? Because all too often it takes only one large loss to obliterate all of the small profits that can be accumulated by using the "profit taking" mentality. It is far, far better to let the profits run.

Here is the strategy for one contract:

1. Assuming setup and trigger are in line, you enter the trade on the close of trading on the entry date. If you are not certain about the trigger having been hit, then wait for the close of trading that day and if the trigger has occurred, then enter on the opening the next day.
2. Place your stop-loss as a close-only order, good till cancelled. If the exchange does not accept a close-only order, then you will need to watch the closing price every day to see if the stop-loss has been penetrated.
3. Make note of the average profit per trade for the trade you are in. This number appears at the lower left of the historical trade listing (i.e., the detailed report).
4. Once this target has been hit, your stop-loss moves to breakeven.

5. If the trade has not been stopped out by the exit date for the trade, then you can:
   (a) Exit on the close at a profit.
   (b) Or hold the position and implement a trailing stop per step 6.
6. Hold the profitable trade with a 75 percent trailing stop (to be explained later in this chapter).

Trading in Units of Two Contracts

If you trade in units of two (i.e., 2, 4, 6, etc.), then you will have much more flexibility. All of the procedures are the same as those for one contract with one addition. You will take profit on one of your positions at the average profit per trade and then raise the stop-loss on the remaining position to breakeven.

Trading in Units of Three Contracts

If you trade in multiples of three (i.e., 3, 6, 9, etc.), then the procedures are exactly as in steps 5a. and 5b. in Trading in One Contract and in units of two contracts with the following additions and changes:

- One third of the position is exited at the average profit per trade.
- The stop-loss on one-third is raised to breakeven.
- The stop-loss on one-third is raised to a trailing stop of 75 percent (to be explained in this section).
- On exit date, one third of the position is closed out if trade is profitable.
- Remaining one third is kept with a trailing stop of 75 percent.

Figure 5.1 is a graphic representation of a trade, along with my notes on entry, exit, and follow-through from start to finish for each of the three methods discussed so far.

Let's begin with a seasonal setup shown in Table 5.1.

As you can see, the trade above meets all five of our setup factors. Figure 5.1 shows the timing chart with my notations and explanations for trading in units of one, two, or three.

Here is my analysis:

- *One contract.* A long was entered on the close of trading 10/27/04, the setup entry date because SI %K has been below 25 percent and was above it. The long entry was on the close at 1128.80. The average profit per trade was 14.906 points. The market did not achieve this target prior to exit date. Price on exit date close was 1130.80. The conservative

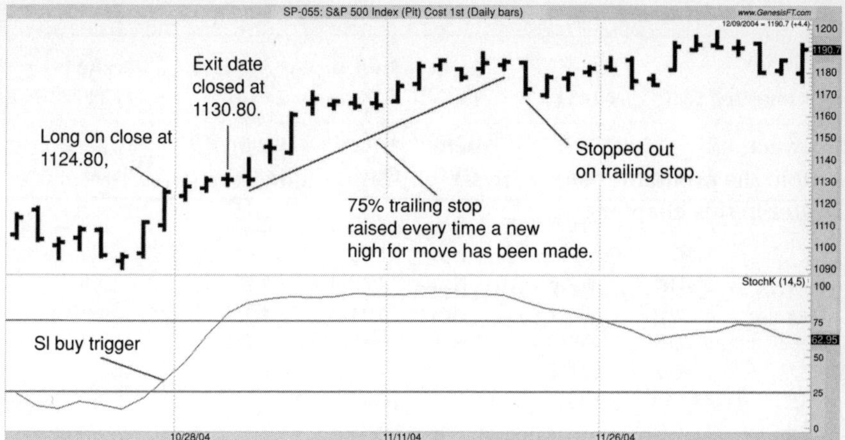

FIGURE 5.1 Seasonal trigger for the S&P trade.
Source: Courtesy of www.GenesisFT.com.

strategy was to close out the trade on the close of trading 11/1/04, the exit date.

RESULT: 6.00 profit (× $250 for the dollar value of the profit).

- *Two units.* If the trade was entered in units of two, then the 6.00 profit was taken on the exit date and the remaining one-half of the position was held using a trailing stop of 75 percent. This means that we were willing to give up no more than 25 percent of the profit. The stop was raised *every time* a new high was made. The second unit would have been closed out at about 1,170 for a considerably higher profit than the first unit.
- *Three units.* If the trade was entered using three units, then one unit would have been closed out at the average profit per trade. However, the average profit per trade was not achieved by the exit date. As a result, two units were closed out on the close of trading on the exit date and a trailing stop of 75 percent would have been used.

SOME IMPORTANT DETAILS

There are some important details that you *must* remember when implementing the seasonal trading strategy discussed in these first five lessons. Far too many traders make careless mistakes. Such mistakes are unacceptable. It is hard enough to make money in the markets. There is no reason to make it more difficult by making careless mistakes.

TABLE 5.1 The Seasonal Trade Setup in S&P Futures

Long Dec S&P		Enter: 10/27	Exit: 11/1	Stop %: 1.50	P/L Ratio: 211.6	Trade #121731308
Contract Year	**Date In**	**Price In**	**Date Out**	**Price Out**	**Profit/ Loss**	**Total**
1982	27-Oct	135.2	1-Nov	137.45	2.25	2.25
1983	27-Oct	167.15	1-Nov	165.6	−1.55	0.7
1984	29-Oct	167.6	1-Nov	170.4	2.8	3.5
1985	28-Oct	188.1	1-Nov	191.2	3.1	6.6
1986	27-Oct	239.2	3-Nov	245.95	6.75	13.35
1987	27-Oct	228.6	2-Nov	257.75	29.15	42.5
1988	27-Oct	279.25	1-Nov	280.15	0.9	43.4
1989	27-Oct	337.2	1-Nov	343.3	6.1	49.5
1990	29-Oct	304	1-Nov	308.45	4.45	53.95
1991	28-Oct	390.6	1-Nov	391.8	1.2	55.15
1992	27-Oct	418	2-Nov	422.05	4.05	59.2
1993	27-Oct	465.7	1-Nov	469.45	3.75	62.95
1994	27-Oct	467.2	1-Nov	469.15	1.95	64.9
1995	27-Oct	583.5	1-Nov	588.25	4.75	69.65
1996	28-Oct	700.35	1-Nov	706.5	6.15	75.8
1997	27-Oct	874	3-Nov	945.7	71.7	147.5
1998	27-Oct	1074.5	2-Nov	1121.2	46.7	194.2
1999	27-Oct	1305.5	1-Nov	1362.5	57	251.2
2000	27-Oct	1401	1-Nov	1431	30	281.2
2001	29-Oct	1073	1-Nov	1082	9	290.2
2002	28-Oct	891.8	1-Nov	898.5	6.7	296.9
2003	27-Oct	1030.7	3-Nov	1054.2	23.5	320.4
2004	27-Oct	1124.8	1-Nov	1130.8	6	326.4
Trades: 23		Winners: 22	Losers: 1		% Winners: 95.65	Daily PF: 2.9813
Avg. Profit: 14.9068		Avg. Loss: −1.55	% Avg. Profit: 2.35		% Avg. Loss: −0.92	Bottom of Form

- When entering a seasonal trade and exiting a seasonal trade on the entry and exit dates do so on the close of trading. This is usually achieved by using a market-on-close (MOC) order. Some traders do not like to use such orders since they believe that bad price executions will be the result. In my experience, it can work both ways—sometimes the fills will be better, sometimes worse. Most often they are reasonable. If you do not want to use a market-on-close order, then you will have to place your orders as market orders in sufficient time to be filled.

- Trailing stop orders are *limit orders* (i.e., orders at a specific price). In other words, they are *not* MOC orders.
- Stop-losses are *stop-close-only orders* (SCO). Some traders do not like these orders because they feel that they result in bad price executions. I disagree.
- If a market is closed on the ideal day of entry or exit, then the trade is executed on the close of trading the next business day.
- If you are uncertain as to whether a trade will trigger on the ideal entry date, then wait until the close of trading to see if there has been a trigger and if there has been one enter on the open the next day.
- Allow a 15 percent leeway of the length of the trade *after* the ideal entry date. Round off all decimals to the next highest day. In other words, if a trade enters on 6/10 and exits 6/20 then the length is 10 days. A 15 percent window is 1.5 days, which rounds up to 2 days.
- The SI indicator I use is based on the calculations from my Genesis Navigator software. Because there are many different ways in which the SI is calculated, you may get slightly different numbers if you use a program other than Genesis to get your SI trigger values. There is nothing that I can suggest to you other than using Genesis. You can learn about the Genesis Navigator charting software at the company's website, http://www.gfds.com.

In a future lesson, I will teach you the Parabolic trading stop because it can be used with other methods.

PRACTICE, PRACTICE, PRACTICE

The most important thing you can do once you have learned the seasonal method is to practice. I strongly suggest that you practice at least 20 trades on paper until you feel comfortable with the method. You can go back into the history at SeasonalTrader.com and see how the trades would have turned out using historical price charts.

REVIEW

Congratulations. You have now completed the first method on your road to trading mastery. In this lesson you learned how to follow-through on seasonal setup and trigger trades using several different strategies depending on position size. In Lesson 6, we begin a new method. The quiz this time is more extensive. Please take your time with it.

LESSON 5 QUIZ

Instructions: This quiz is different from those in the last four lessons. Please take your time with this one and refer to and use Table 5.2 as needed in responding to the questions.

TABLE 5.2 The Seasonal Trade in S&P Futures

Long Dec S&P		**Enter: 10/27**	**Exit: 11/1**	**Stop %: 1.50**	**P/L Ratio: 211.6**	**Trade #121731308**
Contract Year	**Date In**	**Price In**	**Date Out**	**Price Out**	**Profit/ Loss**	**Total**
1982	27-Oct	135.2	1-Nov	137.45	2.25	2.25
1983	27-Oct	167.15	1-Nov	165.6	−1.55	0.7
1984	29-Oct	167.6	1-Nov	170.4	2.8	3.5
1985	28-Oct	188.1	1-Nov	191.2	3.1	6.6
1986	27-Oct	239.2	3-Nov	245.95	6.75	13.35
1987	27-Oct	228.6	2-Nov	257.75	29.15	42.5
1988	27-Oct	279.25	1-Nov	280.15	0.9	43.4
1989	27-Oct	337.2	1-Nov	343.3	6.1	49.5
1990	29-Oct	304	1-Nov	308.45	4.45	53.95
1991	28-Oct	390.6	1-Nov	391.8	1.2	55.15
1992	27-Oct	418	2-Nov	422.05	4.05	59.2
1993	27-Oct	465.7	1-Nov	469.45	3.75	62.95
1994	27-Oct	467.2	1-Nov	469.15	1.95	64.9
1995	27-Oct	583.5	1-Nov	588.25	4.75	69.65
1996	28-Oct	700.35	1-Nov	706.5	6.15	75.8
1997	27-Oct	874	3-Nov	945.7	71.7	147.5
1998	27-Oct	1074.5	2-Nov	1121.2	46.7	194.2
1999	27-Oct	1305.5	1-Nov	1362.5	57	251.2
2000	27-Oct	1401	1-Nov	1431	30	281.2
2001	29-Oct	1073	1-Nov	1082	9	290.2
2002	28-Oct	891.8	1-Nov	898.5	6.7	296.9
2003	27-Oct	1030.7	3-Nov	1054.2	23.5	320.4
2004	27-Oct	1124.8	1-Nov	1130.8	6	326.4
Trades: 23		Winners: 22	Losers: 1		% Winners: 95.65	Daily PF: 2.9813
Avg. Profit: 14.9068		Avg. Loss: −1.55	% Avg. Profit: 2.35		% Avg. Loss: −0.92	Bottom of Form

1. The seasonal setup above meets:
   - **A.** All five factors for a valid setup.
   - **B.** Four of the five factors.
   - **C.** Three of the five factors.
   - **D.** None of the five factors.
2. The ideal seasonal follow up method trades in:
   - **A.** Units of two contracts.
   - **B.** One contract at a time.
   - **C.** Units of three contracts at a time.
   - **D.** Spread trades only.
3. Once a seasonal trade has reached its average profit per trade:
   - **A.** You use a 15 percent trailing stop.
   - **B.** You initiate a spread position.
   - **C.** You look at the stochastic indicator for a new signal.
   - **D.** You raise your stop-loss to breakeven.
4. The correct way to enter a seasonal trade on the entry date is:
   - **A.** To use a market on close order.
   - **B.** Use a stop close only.
   - **C.** Use and MIT order.
   - **D.** Use an OCO order.
5. The trailing stop procedure on seasonal trades is:
   - **A.** Used once a trade has reached its seasonal exit date and remains profitable.
   - **B.** Not a good method.
   - **C.** Uses the stochastic indicator for short term trades.
   - **D.** Is only used by short term speculators.
6. If a market is closed on the ideal date of entry for a seasonal trade then entry occurs:
   - **A.** On the opening of business the next trading day.
   - **B.** Two days after the ideal entry date.
   - **C.** On a 50 percent correction.
   - **D.** On the close of trading the next business day.
7. If a seasonal trade fails to trigger on the ideal entry date then:
   - **A.** You allow the trade 15 percent additional time based on the length of the trade.

   B. The trade is canceled.
   C. You enter a different trade available at SeasonalTrader.com.
   D. You use an MOC order with the parabolic indicator.

8. The reason for holding a winning seasonal trade past the ideal exit date is:
   A. To be greedy.
   B. To maximize profit.
   C. To avoid paying another commission.
   D. To give the stochastic indicator an opportunity to change direction.

LESSON 6, DAY 6

Trading the Power Momentum Formula (PMF)

I consider momentum to be one of the most effective, yet simple indicators that a trader can use. The proper use of *momentum* (from this point on referred to as MOM) can yield a host of benefits, not the least of which is highly precise timing of market entry very close to significant market turning points. This lesson introduces you to my understanding and application of MOM.

MOM provides the following information when used according to my suggestions:

- An evaluation of market strength or weakness.
- An advance indication of a top or bottom.
- An advance indication of trend change.
- Bullish and bearish divergence.
- Timing trigger.
- Trade setup.
- Stop loss and profit target.
- Trailing stop loss.

INTRODUCTION

MOM is a very simple indicator that is easily calculated. MOM is also known as *rate of change* (ROC). Both are essentially the same indicator, but they are derived using different mathematical processes. In order to calculate the five-day MOM of a market, subtract today's price from the price five days ago. The result is a five-day MOM. If today's price is 50, and the price was

60 five days ago, then the five-day MOM is −10. If today's price is 50, and the price five days ago was 40, then today's five-day MOM would be +10.

MOM is a rate change indicator because it provides you with an idea of trend strength. When MOM is moving down very quickly, it is an indication that prices are changing rapidly on the down side with large price moves. When MOM is rising rapidly, it is an indication that the market is trending strongly higher. MOM can be used as a trading indicator by applying some objective rules.

NORMAL AND ABNORMAL RELATIONSHIPS BETWEEN MOM AND PRICE

The *normal* relationship between price and MOM is for them to exhibit parallel trends as well as similar times for highs and lows. They are "in synch" or coordinated most of the time; but when they are not (i.e., out of phase), we can derive valuable information about market strength and/or weakness.

MOM versus price relationships is discussed in this chapter. First, I will illustrate some typical or popular applications of MOM for the purpose of trading. I will show you some very effective applications of MOM while stressing that these are merely applications and *not systems*. I believe that they have considerable potential. But they will require additional rules before they can be considered systems. Remember that we will use the setup, trigger, and follow-through method previously discussed.

Figures 6.1 and 6.2 show normal MOM relationships.

Abnormal Condition 1: Bearish MOM/Price Relationship

Prices Move Higher as Momentum Moves Lower This is a *very* important condition since it is one in which price and MOM diverge from one another. In other words they go in opposite directions. If momentum leads price and if MOM begins to decline while price is moving up then it's a reasonable assumption that at some point in the future price will move *down*.

Unless MOM takes a new direction up, prices are likely to move in the direction of MOM. When the direction of prices and MOM begin to move in opposite directions, the market is telling us that a change in trend is likely. Please remember this rule. I will refer to it again and again.

Rising Price with Falling Momentum Tends to Precede a Top Momentum can be evaluated in any time frame. While most traders use momentum divergence with daily price charts, some want to use weekly or

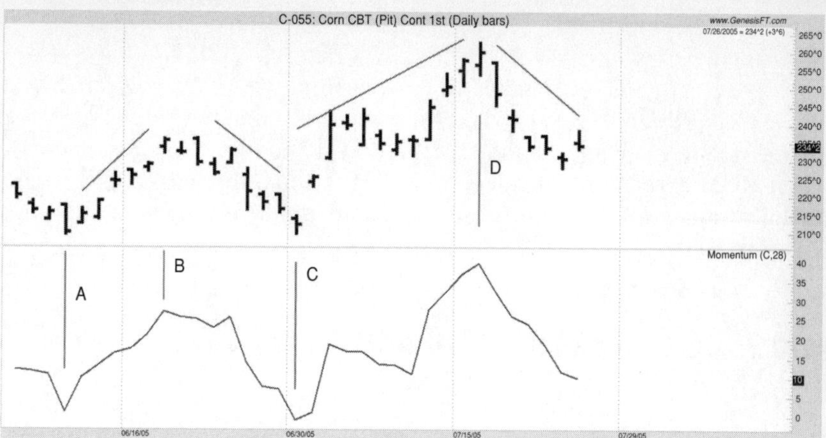

FIGURE 6.1 A normal relationship between price and MOM. As you can see from points A, B, and C, price and MOM were moving in unison, making highs and lows at about the same time.
Source: Courtesy of www.GenesisFT.com.

intraday charts. The rules of application are similar no matter what time frame is being used.

Let's look at a few charts that show this condition in various time frames. Figures 6.3 through 6.5 illustrate this important condition. Please take a few minutes to examine my notes.

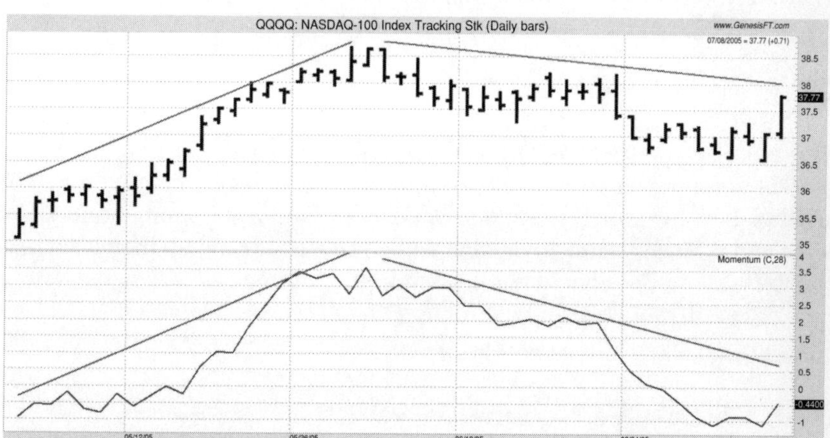

FIGURE 6.2 Similar trends in price and MOM. This is a normal relationship. As prices moved higher so did MOM. As prices moved lower, so did MOM.
Source: Courtesy of www.GenesisFT.com.

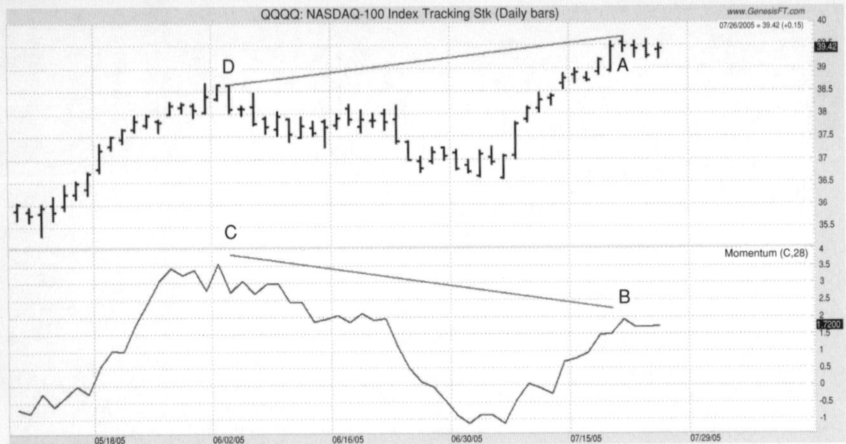

FIGURE 6.3 The Bearish MOM divergence pattern is clear here. Note that as price was making a high at point A, MOM was NOT making a new high at B. The simple rule here is this: If price at A is higher than price at D, while MOM at B is lower than MOM at C, the pattern is BEARISH and a top is likely.
Source: Courtesy of www.GenesisFT.com.

Abnormal Condition 2: Prices Move Lower while MOM Moves Higher: Bullish Divergence

This is a critical condition because it is one in which price and MOM diverge from one another in the opposite direction from the condition previously described (i.e., bearish divergence). In other words, they go in opposite

FIGURE 6.4 This bearish MOM divergence pattern developed on the 30-minute intraday corn chart. Note that AFTER the pattern occurred the price declined sharply and persistently for five days.
Source: Courtesy of www.GenesisFT.com.

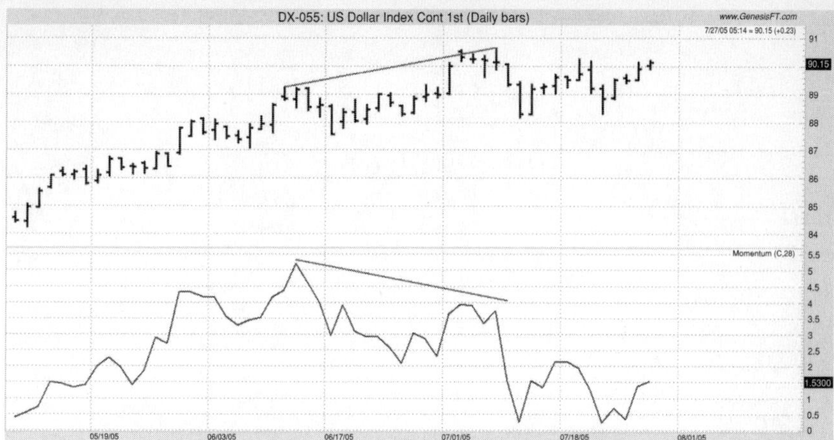

FIGURE 6.5 Bearish MOM divergence pattern in the dollar index futures. This pattern is in the development stage. Remember that these patterns are setups. They must be triggered.
Source: Courtesy of www.GenesisFT.com.

directions. If MOM leads price and if MOM begins to rise while price is moving down, then it is a reasonable assumption that at some point in the future price will move up as it follows MOM. Unless MOM takes a new tack down, prices eventually move in the direction of MOM.

As I stated earlier, when the direction of prices and MOM begin to move in opposite directions, the market is telling us something important about its intended direction. And, we had better listen carefully. Here is another simple rule to remember. Please do not forget this relationship as well because I will refer to it frequently throughout this book.

Falling Price with Rising Momentum Tends to Precede a Low
Figures 6.6 through 6.8 illustrate the bullish condition, which is described in the figure captions that accompany them. Note again that the time frame of the charts, whether daily, weekly, or intraday, is not a factor when evaluating a divergence setup, trigger, or follow-through. The PMF method can be used for stocks as well as futures.

RULES OF APPLICATION

Here are the rules for bullish and bearish MOM setups:

1. Examine the last 60 price bars. In other words, if you use a daily chart, then you will be looking for divergence over the last 60 trading days.

FIGURE 6.6 A bullish MOM setup continues to develop. When you learn the trigger in the next lesson you will see that this market has already triggered a buy signal.
Source: Courtesy of www.GenesisFT.com.

2. There must be at least six price bars inclusive in the pattern. By this I mean that between points A and D (including A and D in the count) there must be six bars (see Figures 6.6 through 6.8).
3. If price low at A is lower than price low at D, while MOM at B is higher than MOM at C, then you have a bullish MOM setup.
4. If price high at A is higher than price high at D, while MOM at B is lower than MOM at C, then you have a bearish MOM setup.

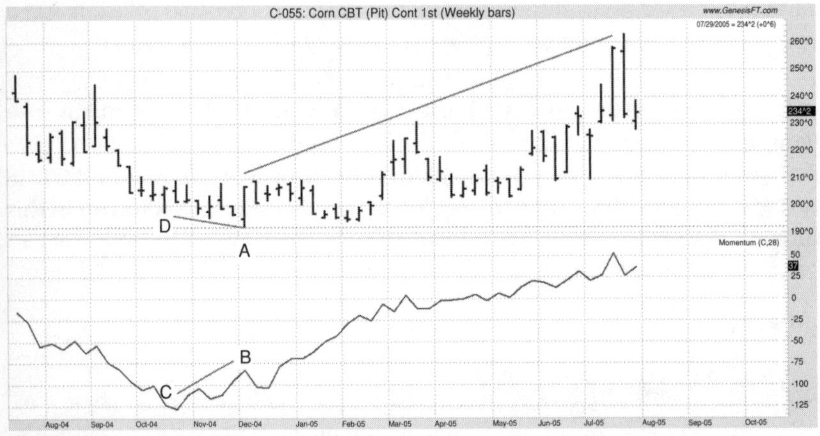

FIGURE 6.7 A weekly bullish MOM setup in corn futures. Note that after the bullish setup developed at points A through D the market moved consistently higher.
Source: Courtesy of www.GenesisFT.com.

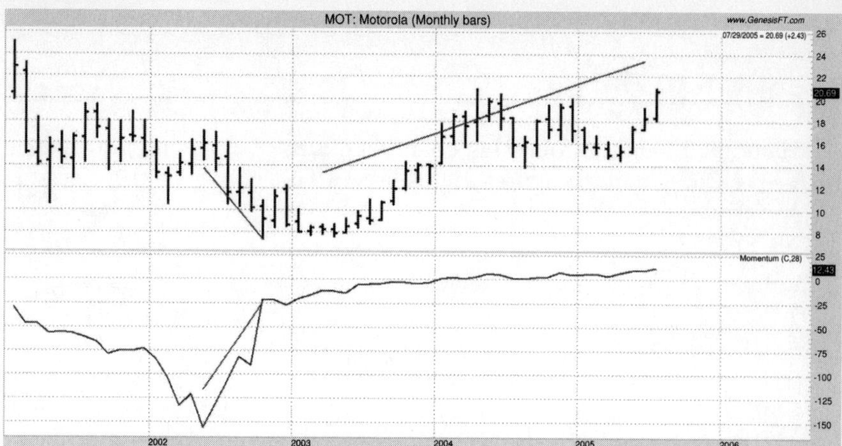

FIGURE 6.8 A monthly bullish MOM pattern in the stock of Motorola. As you can see, the stock moved higher after the pattern developed. Using the trigger method you will see that this one triggered very near the low.
Source: Courtesy of www.GenesisFT.com.

5. You still need a trigger in order to take action.
6. We always use the 28-period MOM for the PMF method.

PRACTICE, PRACTICE, PRACTICE

The most important thing you can do after having learned the MOM method is to practice. Learning to spot these patterns is like learning a new language. I strongly suggest that you practice on at least 50 charts or until you can easily identify MOM divergence.

The quiz for this lesson is visual. In other words, I ask you to draw in any divergence patterns that you see based on the rules given to you in this chapter.

REVIEW

Congratulations! You have now completed the first lesson in your PMF method. You learned how to spot bullish and bearish MOM setups using the momentum indicator.

In Lesson 7 we look at a very simple method for finding MOM divergence setups and triggers.

LESSON 6 QUIZ

Instructions: Using the following charts and a ruler, draw any divergence patterns as shown in the figures in this lesson.

1.

Source: Courtesy of www.GenesisFT.com.

2.

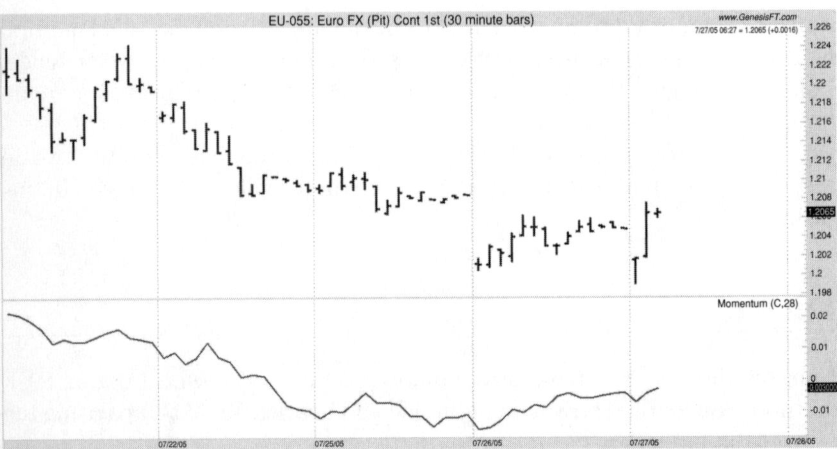

Source: Courtesy of www.GenesisFT.com.

3.

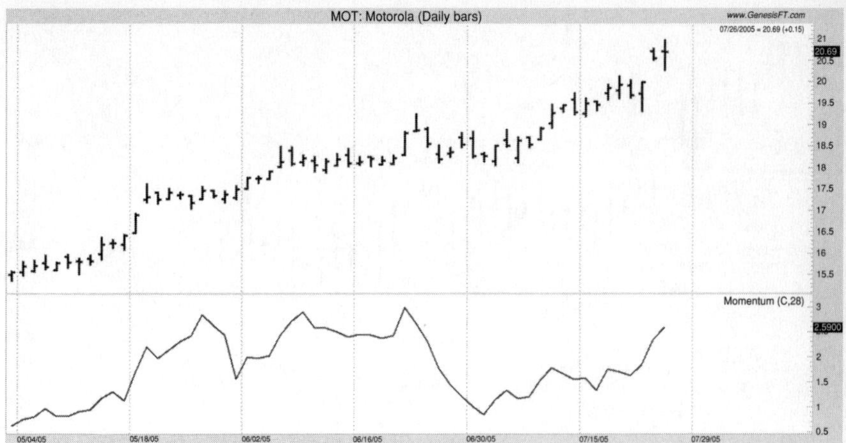

Source: Courtesy of www.GenesisFT.com.

4.

Source: Courtesy of www.GenesisFT.com.

5.

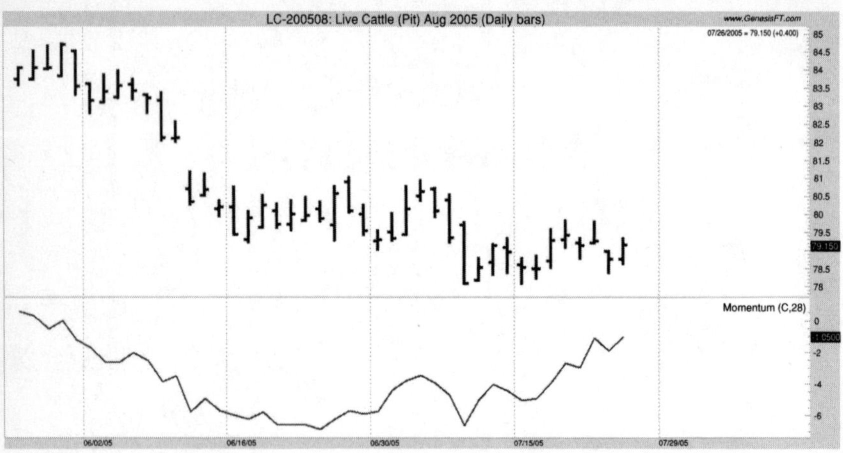

Source: Courtesy of www.GenesisFT.com.

LESSON 7, DAY 7

Power Momentum Formula (PMF) Trigger

In Lesson 1, you learned that there can be no trade without a setup and a trigger. In fact, there can be no trade without a setup, a trigger, *and* a follow-through. This lesson will teach you the PMF trigger. The next lesson will teach you the follow-through.

The *PMF trigger* (PMFT) provides the following information when used according to my suggestions:

- A specific method for timing market entry once there has been a setup.
- The exact point at which to enter a position.
- The best time at which to enter a position.
- A general idea of whether the coming move will be large or small.
- A specific point at which to exit the trade at a profit (next lesson).
- A point at which to exit the trade at loss if necessary (next lesson).
- An initial and trailing profit target.
- An idea of when the trade could trigger (soon or not so soon).

SELL TRIGGER

As you know from the previous lesson, the ability to establish a valid setup is critical to the correct use of the PMF method. Here is a simple "cookbook" method for finding the sell setup and trigger.

1. Look at the last 60 price bars.
2. Find the highest intraday price high.

3. Look at the 28 MOM.
4. Was the highest intraday high accompanied by a new high in MOM +/– five days on either side of the date of the price high?
5. If YES then there is no sell setup.
6. If NO then there is a *sell setup* (SSU).
7. If there is a SSU, then mark your chart as follows:

   A = the new intraday price high
   B = the MOM for the same date as A
   C = the highest MOM previous to B
   D = the intraday price high for the same date as point C

8. Examine your chart. Is the high at A higher than the high at D, while the MOM at B is lower than the MOM at C?
9. If this is true, then find the *lowest* MOM between points B and C inclusive (i.e., including these two points) and mark it with the letter E.
10. If MOM penetrates E at the end of any bar, then you have a sell trigger.

Figure 7.1 shows one example. You will recognize the chart from Lesson 6. I have added the E point.

Figure 7.2 shows another example of a trade that triggered.

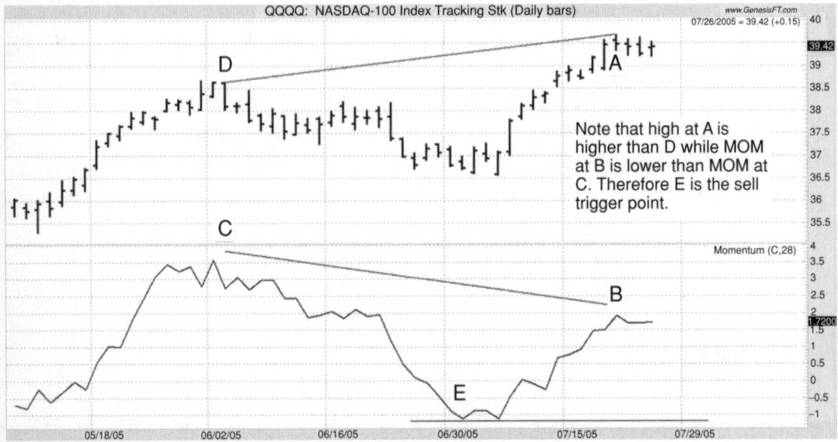

FIGURE 7.1 Bearish MOM divergence pattern is clear here. Note that as price was making a high at point A, MOM was *not* making a new high at B. The sell trigger point at E is clear.
Source: Courtesy of www.GenesisFT.com.

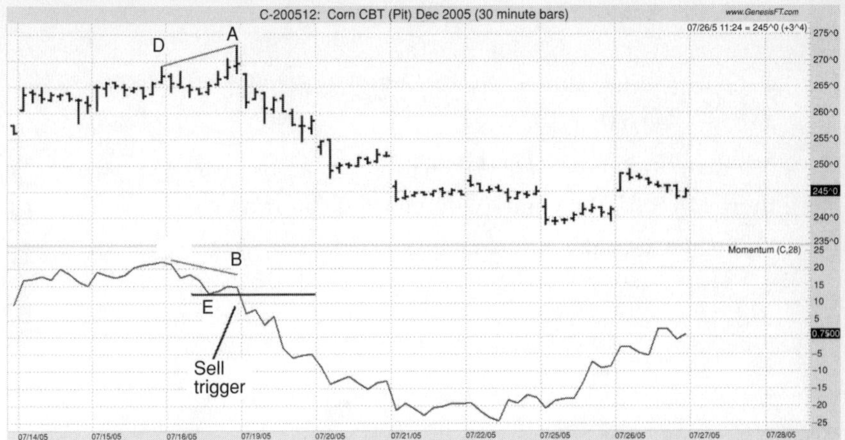

FIGURE 7.2 This bearish MOM divergence pattern developed on the 30-minute intraday corn chart. Note that *after* the sell trigger at E occurred, the price declined sharply and persistently for five days.
Source: Courtesy of www.GenesisFT.com.

BUY TRIGGER

Here is a simple "cookbook" method for finding the buy setup and trigger:

1. Look at the last 60 price bars.
2. Find the lowest intraday price.
3. Look at the 28 MOM.
4. Was the lowest intraday low accompanied by a new low in MOM +/− five days on either side of the date of the price low?
5. If YES then there is no buy setup.
6. If no, then there is a *buy setup* (BSU).
7. If there is a BSU then mark your chart as follows:

   A = the new intraday price low
   B = the MOM for the same date as A
   C = the lowest MOM previous to B
   D = the intraday price low for the same date as point C

8. Examine your chart. Is the low at A lower than the low at D while the MOM at B is higher than the MOM at C?

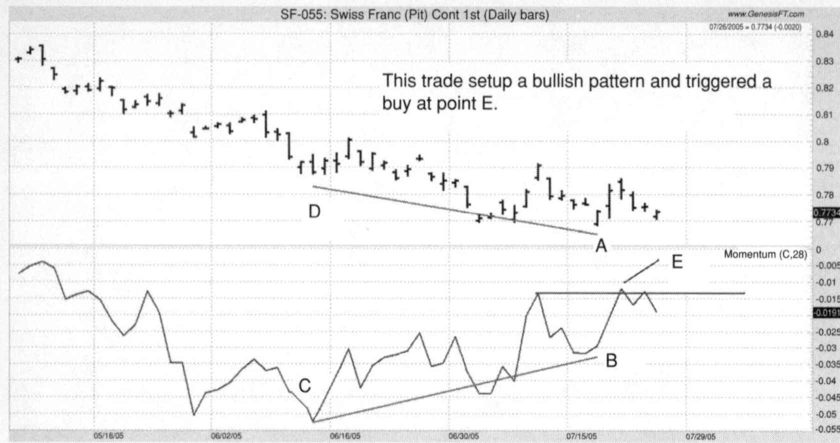

FIGURE 7.3 Here is a bullish MOM setup that has triggered a buy at point E.
Source: Courtesy of www.GenesisFT.com.

9. If this is true, then find the *highest* MOM between points B and C inclusive (for example, including these two points) and mark it with the letter E.
10. If MOM penetrates E at the end of any bar then you have a buy trigger.

Figure 7.3 shows an examples of PMF setup and buy trigger.

Rule-Based Method

The PMF method is 100 percent rule based and it is, therefore, purely objective. A rule-based method is a method that is purely objective. In other words, it requires no interpretation. There are computer software filters that can be used to identify bullish and bearish momentum divergence patterns. These are relatively easy to write. I currently have such a program for Genesis™ clients. It is available to you at no charge. If you would like to download this program and you have Genesis Gold or higher, simply download the special file entitled JBTOOLS. If you do not know how to do this, Genesis technical support can assist you. If you do not have the Genesis™ software you can get a trial version at http://www.genesisft.com.

Because the ability to spot the MD bullish and bearish patterns is critically important to the success of PMF, you must practice as much as possible. The quiz for this lesson includes several more examples and uses the charts from the last lesson.

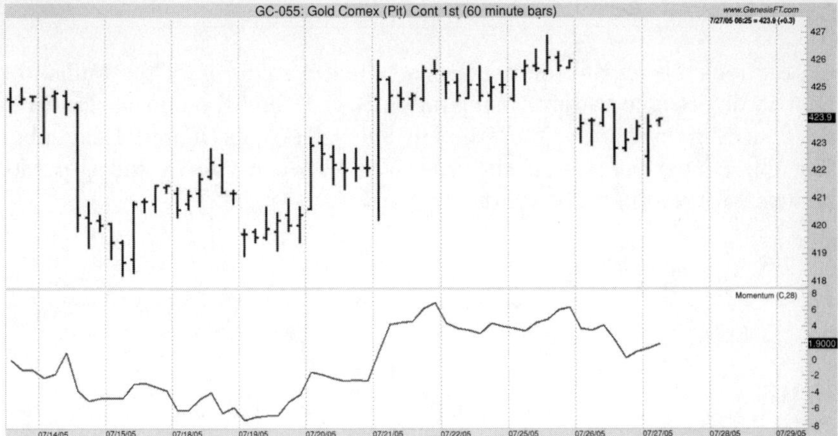

FIGURE 7.4 This chart shows a 60-minute MOM sell setup and trigger in gold futures.
Source: Courtesy of www.GenesisFT.com.

PRACTICE, PRACTICE, PRACTICE

The most important thing you can do after having learned the MOM trigger method is to practice. Learning to spot these patterns is like learning a new language. I strongly suggest you practice on at least 50 charts in order to find the setup and the trigger until you can easily identify MOM divergence and the trigger point visually. If you are uncertain about your work, please feel free to e-mail me a chart with your work and I will examine it for you. Be sure to include your e-mail address.

The quiz for this lesson is visual. I will ask you to draw in any divergence patterns and triggers you see based on the rules given to you here and in the previous lesson.

REVIEW

Congratulations. You have now completed the first lesson in your PMF method. You learned how to identify the trigger point (E point) for bullish and bearish MOM setups using the MOM indicator. The lesson outlines a step-by-step or "cookbook" procedure for finding and identifying the trigger point.

In Lesson 8, we look at a very simple but comprehensive method for adding follow-through to the MOM divergence setups and triggers.

LESSON 7 QUIZ

Instructions: Using the following charts and a ruler, mark the bullish or bearish divergence patterns using the A, B, C, D, and E points as shown in the figures in this lesson. Mark the buy and sell signals (if any). Remember that there must be at least six price bars between your A and D points inclusive for a setup to be valid.

1.

Source: Courtesy of www.GenesisFT.com.

2.

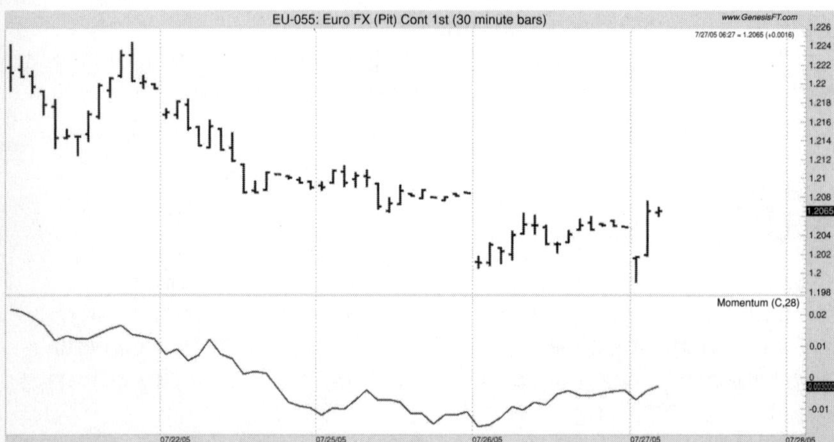

Source: Courtesy of www.GenesisFT.com.

3.

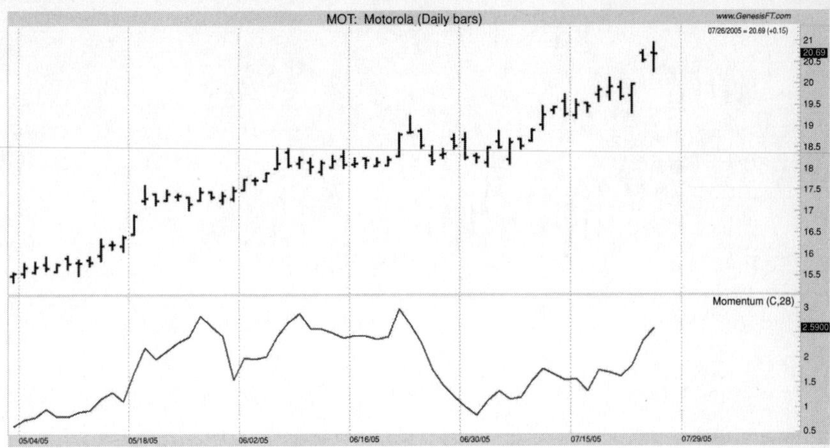

Source: Courtesy of www.GenesisFT.com.

4.

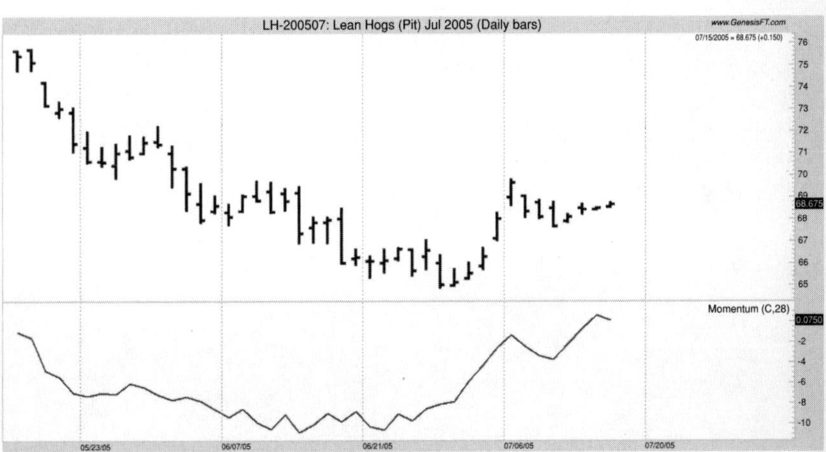

Source: Courtesy of www.GenesisFT.com.

5.

Source: Courtesy of www.GenesisFT.com.

LESSON 8, DAY 8

PMF Follow-through: Part I

As you know from my explanation of the STF method, there can be no trade for us without a setup, a trigger, and follow-through. In the previous lesson, you learned how to find the setup as well as the trigger. This lesson teaches you the PMF follow-through.

As you recall every valid trading approach involves three parts, the setup, the trigger, and follow-through. This lesson shows you how we follow-through on the PMF method. The next lesson shows you how the follow-through method can be used in various profit-maximizing strategies.

The PMF follow-through method provides the following information when used according to my suggestions:

- A specific method for follow-through of a trade once there has been a setup and a trigger.
- The exact initial profit target after a trigger has occurred.
- How and when to trail stop losses.
- A general idea of whether the move will be large or small.
- A specific point at which to exit the trade at the full profit target.
- A point at which to exit the trade at loss if necessary.
- The number of contracts (or shares) to trade.

CALCULATING THE PROFIT TARGET

In Lesson 7, you learned that the ability to establish a valid setup and trigger are critically important to the correct use of the PMF method. Once this has been done, the next step is to use correct and effective follow-through. Here is the step-by-step method for determining follow-through on PMF trades:

1. After the trigger has been hit and you have entered a trade, find the highest intraday high and the lowest intraday low between points A and D.
2. Calculate the difference between these two prices.
3. Calculate 50 percent of the difference. You now have the first profit target (PT1).
4. If you have a long position, *add* the price of the market on the trigger date to PT1 to get your exact profit target.
5. If you have a short position, *subtract* the price of the market on the trigger date from PT1 to get your exact profit target.
6. The full profit target (PT2) is the full range of the difference you calculated.
7. Depending on the number of contracts or shares you have entered, the exit strategy will vary.

Figures 8.1 through 8.4 show several examples with explanations of this procedure using charts that you should already be familiar with from previous PMF lessons. Carefully study my notations on the charts. Figures 8.3 and 8.4 show the complete procedure from setup through initial follow-through.

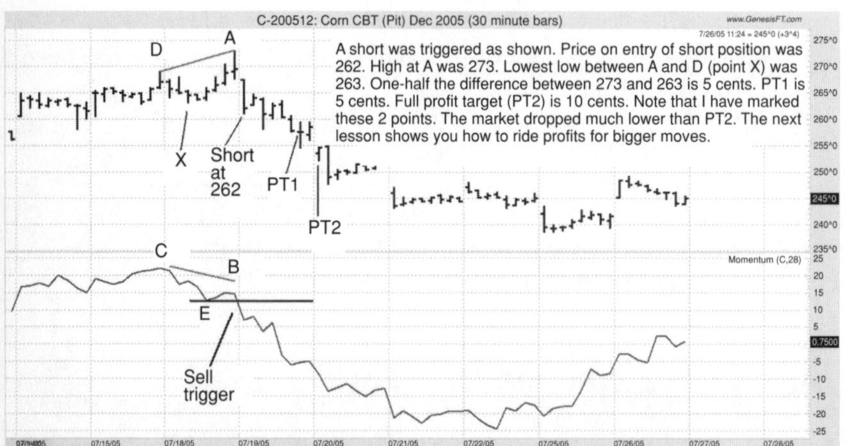

FIGURE 8.1 Here is a PMF trade with setup, trigger, and follow-through.
Source: Courtesy of www.GenesisFT.com.

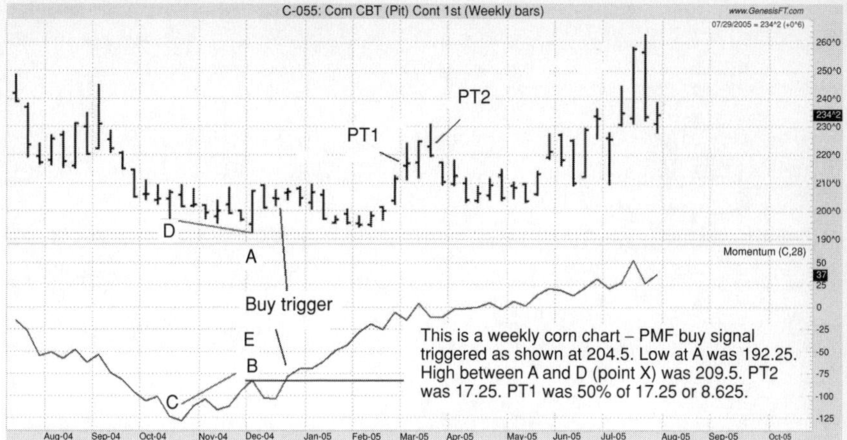

FIGURE 8.2 This trade also triggered and followed through as noted.
Source: Courtesy of www.GenesisFT.com.

PRACTICE

I have stated, perhaps overstated, that the most important thing you can do after having learned the MOM trigger method is to practice. This is even

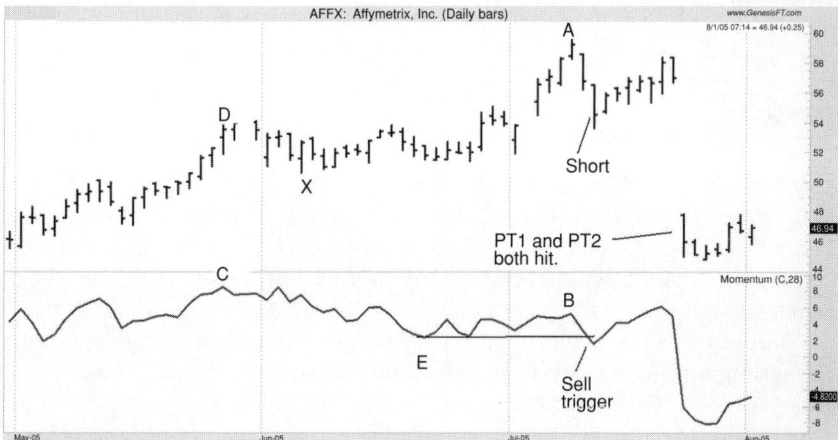

FIGURE 8.3 This stock established a bearish pattern (A–D and C–B), which was triggered at E. A short position entered as shown at 54.53. The range between A and D was 59.73 to 50.56 or 9.17. PT1 was, therefore, about 4.56, which, when subtracted from the entry price was 49.97 and the full target price was 45.36. Both targets were achieved on the same date when the stock dropped sharply.
Source: Courtesy of www.GenesisFT.com.

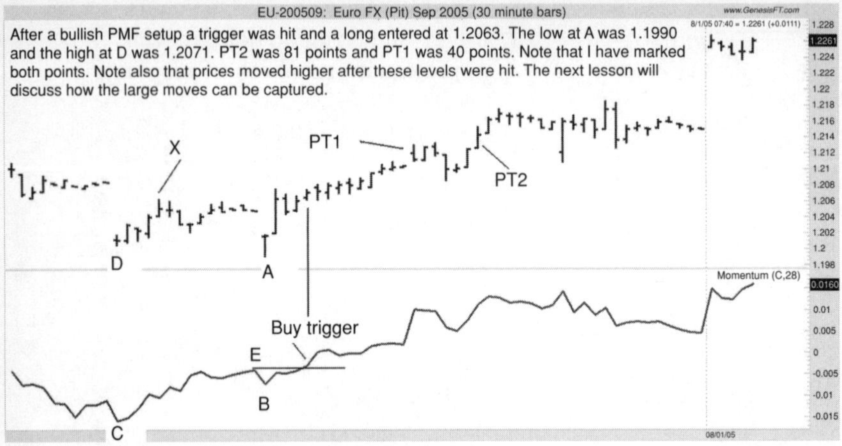

EU-200509: Euro FX (Pit) Sep 2005 (30 minute bars)
www.GenesisFT.com
After a bullish PMF setup a trigger was hit and a long entered at 1.2063. The low at A was 1.1990 and the high at D was 1.2071. PT2 was 81 points and PT1 was 40 points. Note that I have marked both points. Note also that prices moved higher after these levels were hit. The next lesson will discuss how the large moves can be captured.
X
PT1
PT2
D
A
Buy trigger
E
B
C
Momentum (C,28)
08/01/05

FIGURE 8.4 This is yet another example of the complete process through initial follow-through. Note that prices continued higher after exit. The next chapter will show you several methods for capturing such moves.
Source: Courtesy of www.GenesisFT.com.

more important now that you know the setup, trigger, and initial follow-through.

The quiz for this lesson is visual. As with Lesson 7, I ask you to draw in any divergence patterns and triggers you see based on the rules given to you in this lesson and in the previous lesson.

REVIEW

You have now completed the first lesson in your PMF method. In this lesson, you learned how to identify the trigger point (E point) for bullish and bearish MOM setups using the MOM indicator. The lesson outlines a step-by-step or "cookbook" procedure for finding and identifying the trigger point.

In Lesson 8 we will look at a very simple but comprehensive method for adding follow-through to the MOM divergence setups and triggers.

LESSON 8 QUIZ

Instructions: Using the following charts and a ruler, mark the bullish or bearish divergence patterns using the A, B, C, D, and E points shown in the figures in this lesson. Mark any buy and sell signals (if any). Then mark the approximate first and second profit targets. Since you do not have the actual price lows and highs, you can use approximate numbers in responding to this quiz.

1.

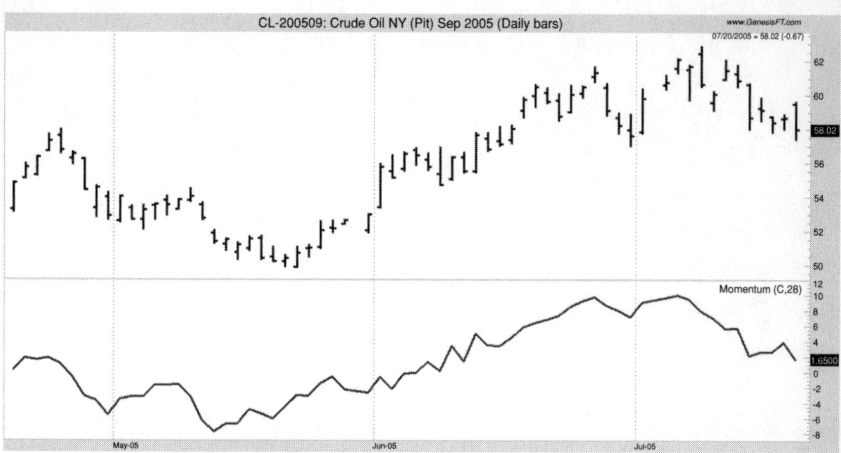

Source: Courtesy of www.GenesisFT.com.

2.

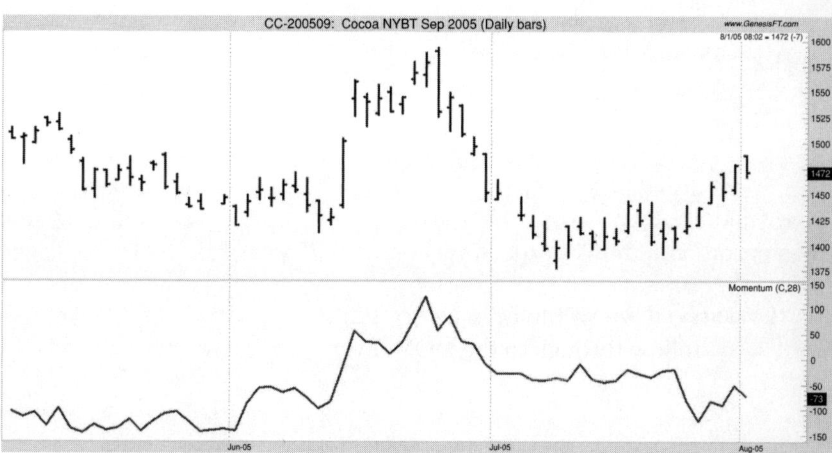

Source: Courtesy of www.GenesisFT.com.

3.

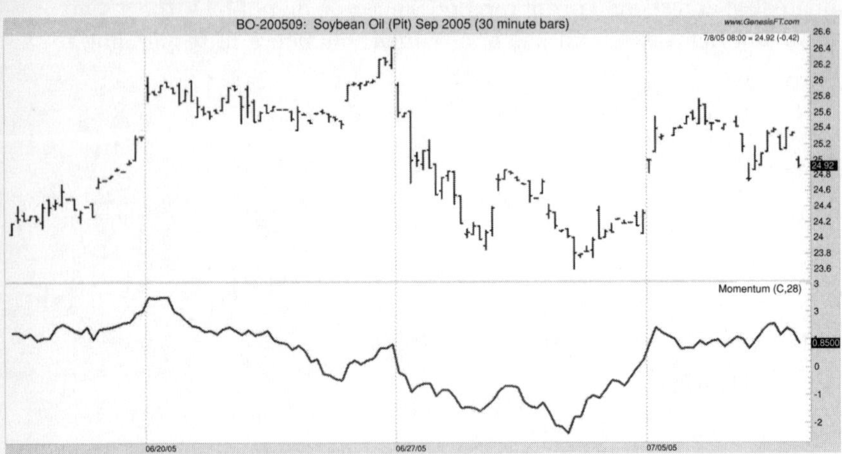

Source: Courtesy of www.GenesisFT.com.

4.

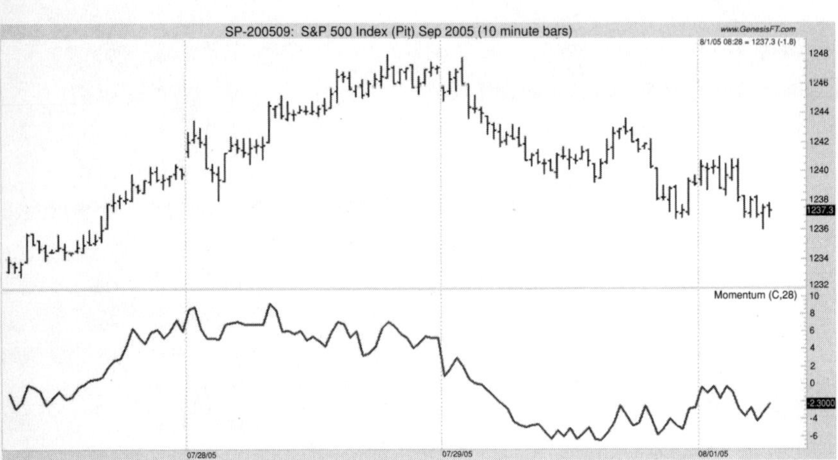

Source: Courtesy of www.GenesisFT.com.

5.

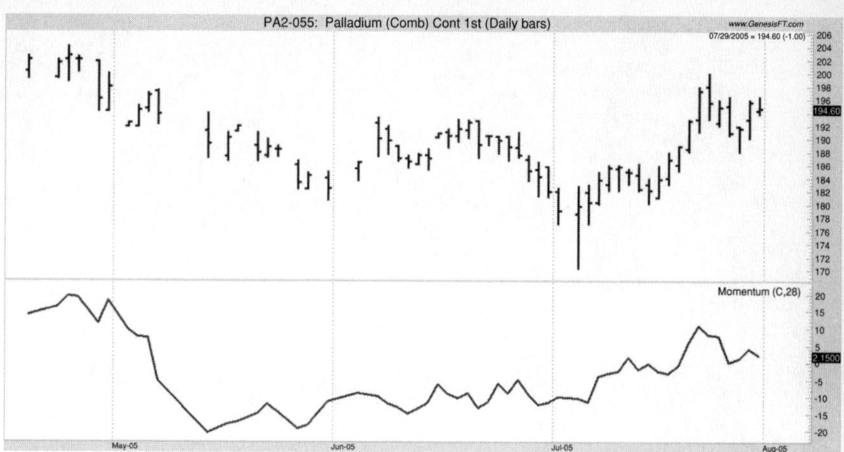

Source: Courtesy of www.GenesisFT.com.

6.

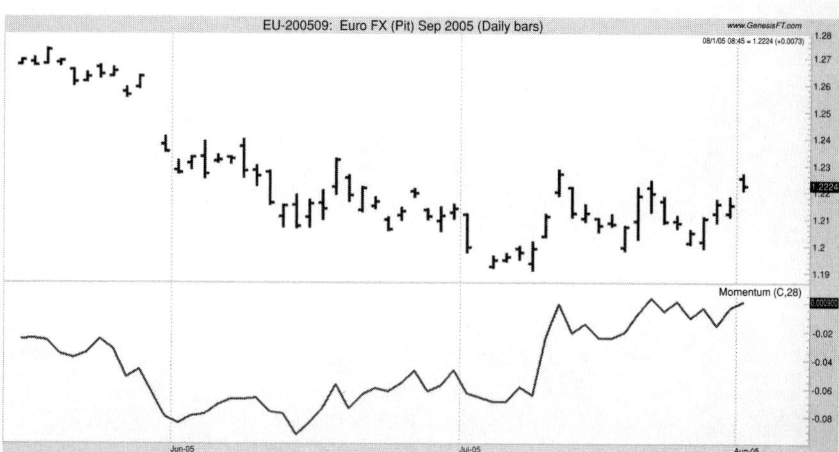

Source: Courtesy of www.GenesisFT.com.

LESSON 9, DAY 9

PMF Follow-through: Part II

The last few lessons gave you a specific explanation of the STF structure that is part of the PMF method. As you well know by now, every trade requires a setup, a trigger, and follow-through. This is true for the PMF method as well as every method I will teach you. Unless you plan to use luck as your trading system, you will not fare well. If you follow the STF structure no matter what your trading methodology may be, your odds of success will improve substantially.

In Lessons 7 and 8 I taught you how to find the setup as well as the trigger and initial follow-through. This lesson will teach you the PMF full follow-through method that is designed to maximize your profits by letting the big winners run. The full follow-through method gives you the following information:

- A specific method for determining the initial stop-loss for a trade once there has been a setup and a trigger.
- The exact procedure for different position sizes.
- How and when to trail stop-losses.
- A general idea of whether the move will be large or small.
- A specific method for trailing a stop-loss when trades make explosive moves in your favor.
- A conservative, aggressive, and professional follow-up approach depending on your account size and degree of risk tolerance.

REVIEW OF THE METHOD

From the previous two lessons, recall that the PMF method is fully objective. It is based on a step-by-step procedure. The only way to achieve consistency in your trading is by following the steps. The only way to learn from your mistakes is to know where you may have gone wrong.

There are two types of losing trades—the *unavoidable loss* and the *dumb loss*. The unavoidable loss occurs when a method loses money simply because not all methods are right all the time. The dumb loss occurs when you make a mistake in applying the method. The dumb loss is a loss that you made due to your own ignorance, lack of discipline, or lack of organization. The dumb loss is unacceptable. The only way you can learn how and when you took a dumb loss is by looking over your procedures. Here are the specific procedures for PMF:

1. Find the PMF setup.
2. Determine the buy or sell trigger point.
3. Enter the trade once it has triggered.
4. A trigger can only occur at the *end* of a price bar—do not sit and watch the trigger within the time frame of the price bar—it is a waste of time and will drive you nuts.
5. If you are certain that a trade has triggered at the end of a price bar, then enter on the close of the bar. If you are not certain (i.e., the MOM value is too close to the trigger point), then wait for the bar to close and if there is a trigger then enter on the OPEN of the next bar.

The exact procedure from this point forward depends on your position size. There are three levels of position size, each of which depends on your degree of risk tolerance and account size.

CONSERVATIVE STRATEGY

The conservative strategy is simple. For the futures trader, it involves trading in one contract of the given market or 100 shares (round lot) of a stock. Many traders have asked me if I recommend options as a substitute for a position in futures or stocks.

My answer is no. The problem with options is that the price executions are often very poor, liquidity is often what accounts for poor price executions, and they lose time value. Instead, I advise trading the PMF method for futures, futures spreads and/or stocks.

The conservative trader has three choices when using the PMF method. Here are the choices and their pros and cons:

- *Place a profit taking order at PT1.* The good news is that you often make a profit because PT1 is frequently hit. The bad news is that if the market keeps moving in the given direction, you will leave a lot of money on the table. The worse news is that you may make as many as 10 small profits in a row but, take my word for it, you could give it all back plus more on one losing trade. I do not recommend this strategy.
- *When PT1 is hit, change your stop-loss to breakeven (i.e., the price at which you entered).* See the seasonal Lessons 2 and 3 or a more thorough description of the breakeven stop. The good news is that you are giving the market plenty of room to reach PT2 or even better levels. The bad news is that you may get stopped out at breakeven many times. And this will make you mad. Unfortunately, as a one-contract trader, you do not have a choice. If you trade PMF in stocks, you could split your 100 shares into three units and use the *aggressive* strategy described below.
- The best strategy for conservative traders is to place a stop-loss at breakeven when PT1 is hit and then to use the TS (trailing stop) procedure when PT2 has been hit (see trailing stop procedures below).

MODERATE STRATEGY

This follow-through method requires you to trade in units of two. If you trade futures, then you will trade either 2, 4, 6, 8, . . . contracts. If you trade stocks, then you will trade 200, 400, 600, 800, . . . shares. You will exit your positions as follows:

1. After entering your position, you will place a profit taking order at PT1 to exit ~HF (high frequency) of your position.
2. When PT1 is hit, you raise your stop-loss breakeven on the remaining ~HF of your position.
3. When PT2 is hit you will begin to trail a stop at 50 percent.
4. If a trade produces an open profit of twice PT2 implement a 75 percent trailing stop.

AGGRESSIVE STRATEGY

This follow-through method requires you to trade in units of three. If you trade futures you'll trade either 3, 6, 9,... contracts. If you trade stocks, then you will trade 300, 600, 900,... shares. You will exit your positions as follows:

1. After entering your position, you will place a profit-taking order at PT1 on one-third of your position.
2. When PT1 is hit, you will raise your stop-loss breakeven on one-third of your position with a stop-loss that locks in 50 percent of your profit on another one-third of your position.
3. When PT2 is hit you will exit another one-third of your position unless stopped out.
4. When PT2 is hit and you have closed out one-third of your position, you will trail a stop on the remaining one-third of the position.
5. If a trade produces an open profit of twice PT2, implement a 75 percent trailing stop.

The aggressive strategy allows you to take a profit, to trail a stop, and to hold a position for the bigger move should it occur. The moderate strategy also allows for this possibility. The conservative strategy can also allow you to ride a trade past PT1 and PT2; however, you will not be able to enjoy the benefits of taking some profits. It would be an "all or nothing" strategy for the conservative trader. As you can imagine, this is anathema to the small trader who is intent on taking profits as often as possible. If you use the conservative strategy, you fare better in the long run than if you trade for the bigger moves.

Naturally, the decision is yours. But I think you substantially increase your odds of success by going after the big moves rather than the small moves.

EXAMPLES

Figures 9.1 and 9.2 show two detailed examples of PMF trades from start to finish with all three strategies. Note that the procedure is the same for futures and stocks. The only difference is in the vehicle that is being used.

STOP-LOSSES AND THE DANGER ZONE

Now let us look at the PMF stop-loss. Most traders tell you that your stop-loss should be placed at a level that you can afford. This is nonsense. The

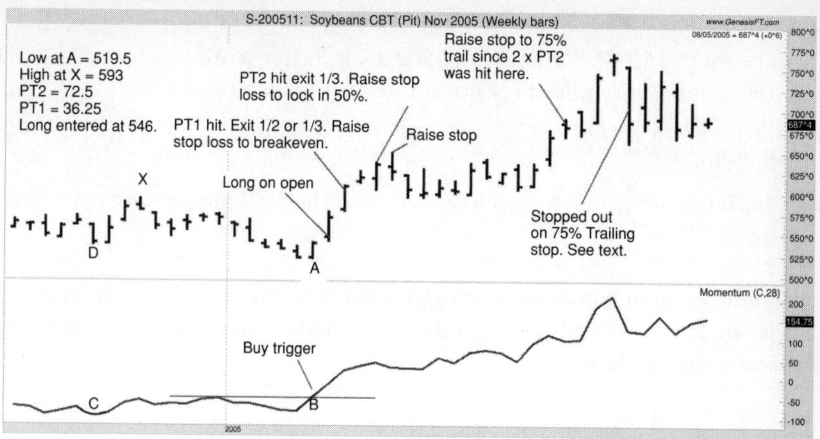

FIGURE 9.1 A PMF trade with setup, trigger and initial follow-through.
Source: Courtesy of www.GenesisFT.com.

market does not give a darn about what *you* can afford to risk. Stop-losses must be dynamic and system related. Your stop-loss should be a function of the market and/or the system.

The PMF initial stop-loss procedure is simple:

1. Stop-loss on long position is based on MOM. If MOM closes below point C, then you exit the trade.
2. Stop-loss on short position is based on MOM. If MOM closes above point C, then you exit your position.

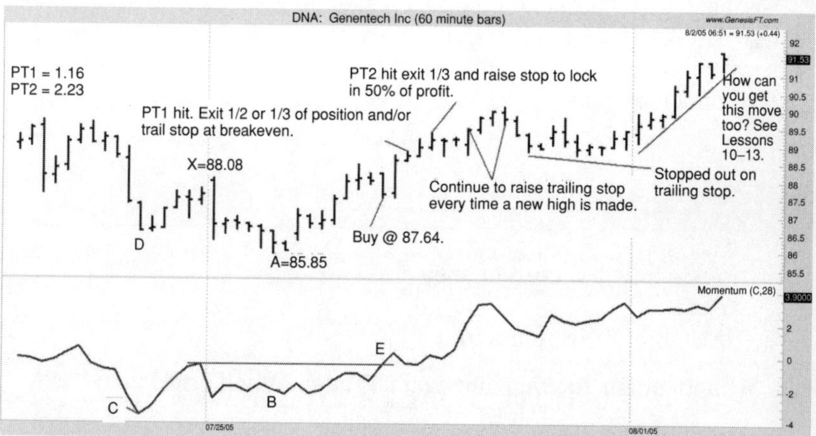

FIGURE 9.2 This trade triggered and followed through as noted.
Source: Courtesy of www.GenesisFT.com.

3. You can get an estimate of what your stop-loss should be initially by working the MOM formula backwards. In other words, determine what price would be required for point C to be penetrated.
4. You are in the *danger zone* (i.e., risk of being stopped out at a loss) until PT1 is hit.
5. Another more precise stop loss is to use the PT2 amount as your stop-loss.

If you are not clear on how to calculate the approximate risk send based on the point C penetration, send me an e-mail at jake@trade-futures.com and I will tell you how.

PRACTICE, PRACTICE, PRACTICE

I want to emphasize again that the most important thing you can do after having learned the MOM trigger method is to practice. This is even more important now that you know the setup, trigger, and full follow-through.

REVIEW

In this lesson you learned how to manage the risks and rewards in the PMF method for three different levels of risk tolerance. You also learned the proper stop-loss procedures.

You have now completed the first lesson in your PMF method. In Lesson 10 we look at Part 1 of my *Moving Average Channel* (MAC) to see how it can work as a trend indicator, timing indicator, and support/resistance swing trading method.

LESSON 9 QUIZ

Instructions: Circle the correct answers.

1. The DANGER ZONE refers to:

   A. What happens to you when you use any method other than PMF.

   B. A margin call.

   C. The time you are in a PMF trade prior to PT1 being hit.

   D. Any time you trade options.

2. The 75 percent trailing stop is implemented when:

   A. Twice PT2 has been hit.
   B. You get concerned about a trade.
   C. Your broker calls you.
   D. You have made at least $400 profit on a trade.

3. PT1 is:

   A. The term used for an aggressive portfolio method.
   B. A method for triggering spread trades.
   C. The stop-loss for all PMF trades.
   D. One half of PT2.

4. The aggressive PMF strategy is:

   A. To trade options and futures in a diversified portfolio.
   B. To trade units of three for futures and 300 shares for stocks.
   C. To use no stop-losses until PT3 is hit.
   D. To double up your position at PT1.

5. If MOM closes above point C after triggering a PMF sell:

   A. Call your broker and ask for a refund.
   B. Add PT1 and PT2 and place a trailing stop of 75 percent.
   C. Spread your position into a related market.
   D. Exit the trade since the stop-loss has been hit.

6. The conservative strategy for PMF:

   A. Is not recommended under any circumstances.
   B. Is for nervous traders only.
   C. Is best used as if the one unit was the 3rd unit so as to maximize profits.
   D. Is recommended for options traders only.

7. The aggressive strategy for PMF is:

   A. The best way to capture major profits.
   B. To use no stop-loss.
   C. Worthless unless you have a PhD in economics.
   D. Only for new traders.

8. To calculate PT1 and PT2:

A. Take the difference of the highest high and the lowest low between points A and D inclusive.

B. Use a Gann Angle calculator.

C. Use Fibonacci numbers.

D. Use the Black-Scholes options pricing model.

LESSON 10, DAY 10

Using the Moving Average Channel: Part I

The *moving average channel* (MAC) is a method I have developed and refined over 20 years ago. It is very useful and effective in stocks and futures. It offers:

- A specific method for determining the initial stop-loss for a trade once there has been a setup and a trigger.
- The exact procedure for different position sizes.
- How and when to trail stop-losses.
- A general idea of whether the move will be large or small.
- A specific method for trailing a stop-loss when trades make explosive moves in your favor.
- A conservative, aggressive, and professional follow-up approach depending on your account size and degree of risk tolerance.

THE METHOD

The MAC is based on moving averages of highs and lows, as opposed to the use of traditional moving average crossover systems, which use the *moving average* (MA) of closing prices The MAC uses two MAs, one of the high price and one of the low prices. In so doing, the MAC is quite different than traditional moving averages and it is not subject to many of the same limitations that inhibit the performance results with traditional moving averages. Typical results with MA-based systems that use closing prices are very poor, usually in the range of 30 percent to 45 percent accuracy. The MAC improves the odds considerably because it is a total method that uses my STF (setup, trigger, and follow-through) approach.

Here are the rules of application for the MAC:

- Calculate an eight-period simple MA of the low price for each bar (i.e., daily or weekly or intraday).
- Calculate a 10-period simple MA of the high price for each bar (i.e., daily or weekly or intraday).
- A *buy* setup occurs when *one* complete bar occurs above the *moving average of the high* (MAH).
- A BUY trigger occurs when a second consecutive complete bar occurs above the MAH.
- A SELL setup occurs when one complete bar occurs below the *moving average of the low* (MAL).
- A SELL trigger occurs when a second consecutive complete bar occurs below the MAL.

Very important! The price bars must be completely above or below the MA line to be valid. Please note this carefully—the *entire* bar must be outside the channel.

Note that these are the basic rules. The next lesson will go into considerably greater detail regarding the many effective uses of the MAC. See Figure 10.1 for an example of a daily futures chart and Figure 10.2 for an example on a stock chart.

IT LOOKS EASY

The two examples I cited make the MAC seem easy; but there is a lot more to the MAC than what I have shown you to this point. Here are a few more very important aspects of the MAC:

- When the MAC has triggered a buy, the MA of the low serves as support in the new uptrend.
- When the MAC has triggered a sell, the MA of the high serves as resistance in the new downtrend.
- The more consecutive bars that comprise a new signal, the more significant the new trend is likely to be.

FIGURE 10.1 The MAC on a daily chart of Swiss Franc futures showing setup, trigger, and follow-through.
Source: Courtesy of www.GenesisFT.com.

- A narrowing channel in an uptrend tends to precede a correction down or a possible top.
- A widening channel in an uptrend tends to precede a sharp rally.
- A narrowing channel in a downtrend tends to precede a correction up or a possible bottom.
- A widening channel in a downtrend tends to precede a sharp decline.

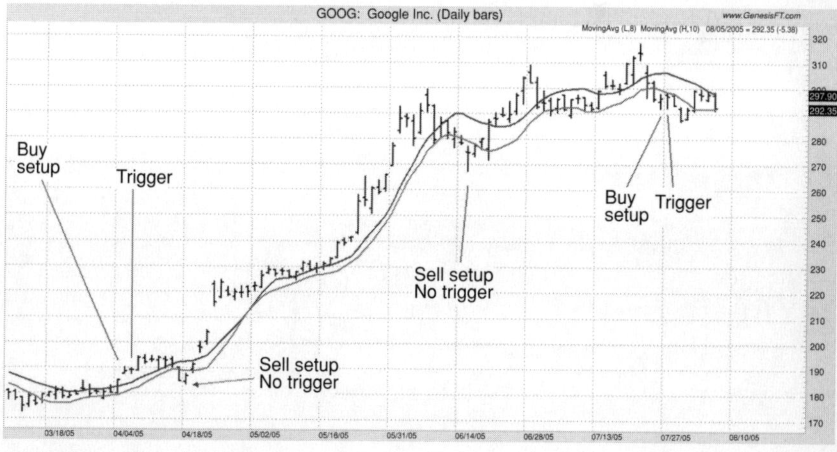

FIGURE 10.2 The MAC on a daily chart of Google (GOOG) stock showing setup and trigger.
Source: Courtesy of www.GenesisFT.com.

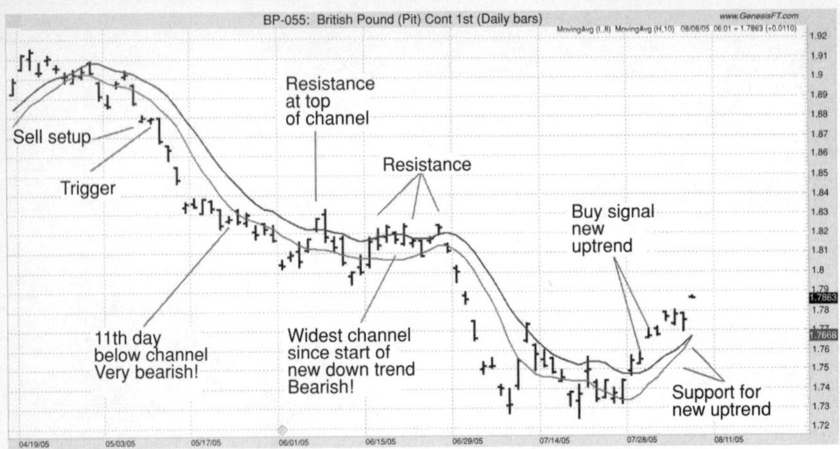

FIGURE 10.3 The MAC on a daily chart of British pound futures showing setup, trigger, and result.
Source: Courtesy of www.GenesisFT.com.

All of these are discussed in detail in Lesson 11. Figures 10.3 and 10.4 show annotated examples of these conditions.

PRACTICE, PRACTICE, PRACTICE

Now that you have learned the basics of the MAC, it is time to practice. Spend some time with the MAC. You will find that in a "choppy" market it

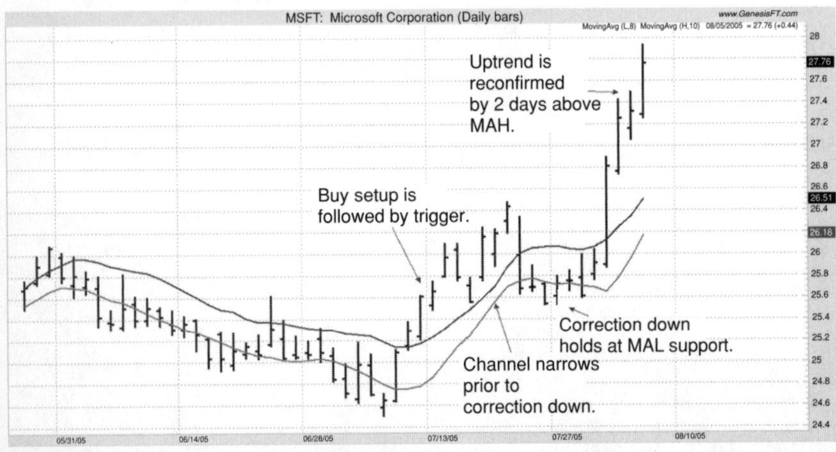

FIGURE 10.4 The MAC on a daily chart of Microsoft (MSFT) stock showing setup, trigger, and result.
Source: Courtesy of www.GenesisFT.com.

has some "issues" that seem to decrease performance. In the next lesson, I show you several ways to rectify those situations.

REVIEW

In this lesson you learned about the MAC method, which consists of two MAs. The MAC uses a 10-period MA of the highs and an eight-period MA of the lows. The MAC triggers for a buy and a sell were discussed. The MAC also provides a way of determining support, resistance, and strength of trend.

Congratulations! You have now completed the first lesson in your MAC method. In Lesson 11, we will look at Part 2 of my Moving Average Channel (MAC) to see more specifically how it can work as a trend indicator, timing indicator, and support/resistance swing trading method.

LESSON 10 QUIZ

Instructions: Circle the correct answers.

1. The MAC is
   - **A.** A method that uses two moving averages, one of the lows and one of the highs.
   - **B.** A method for trading meat and livestock futures.
   - **C.** Is a risk management method called "Managed Account Concept."
   - **D.** None of the above.
2. In order for a price bar to be valid, either as a setup or a trigger it must:
   - **A.** Close higher than it opened.
   - **B.** Use the 14 period slow stochastic.
   - **C.** Occur within 6 days of the last signal.
   - **D.** Be completely outside the channel.
3. When the MAC widens in an uptrend this tends to indicate:
   - **A.** The end of a bull market.
   - **B.** The start of a bear market.
   - **C.** That the market will likely move sharply higher.
   - **D.** That the commercials are not in the market at this time.

4. The more consecutive bars above the channel:
   - **A.** The less likely the market is to rally.
   - **B.** The more the odds favor a large up move.
   - **C.** Lower the trading volume.
   - **D.** The greater the odds of a seasonal decline.
5. In a declining market after a sell trigger:
   - **A.** The MAL serves as resistance.
   - **B.** The MAH cannot be used for triggers.
   - **C.** The MAH serves as approximate resistance.
   - **D.** The channel is not useful.
6. When the MAC becomes very narrow in an uptrend:
   - **A.** The odds have turned 50/50 for a rally.
   - **B.** A seasonal buy signal is likely with the PMF method.
   - **C.** A correction down to support is likely.
   - **D.** It means that open interest is rising.
7. The MAC uses:
   - **A.** Exponential moving averages.
   - **B.** Weighted moving averages.
   - **C.** Gann angles.
   - **D.** None of the above.
   - **E.** All of the above.

LESSON 11, DAY 11

Using the Moving Average Channel: Part II

Lesson 10 discussed the MAC basic aspects. In this lesson, we finalize application of this method in its various forms. Note that the MAC is very versatile. It can be used in at least five different ways. I urge you to study my suggested applications and then decide on which of them to fit your needs best.

The moving average channel (MAC) can be used for swing trading consistent with the trend. The rules are as follows:

- If the MAC trend is up, then buy at the moving average of the low (MAL) and take profit at the moving average of the high (MAH) or implement a trailing stop once you have achieved your initial profit target—the MAH.
- If the MAC trend is down, then sell at the MAH and take profit at the MAL or implement a trailing stop once the profit target has been hit.

MAC APPLICATION AS A TREND INDICATOR AND TREND CHANGE INDICATOR

The simplest application of the MAC is to use it as a trend and trend change indicator.

The rules are as follows:

- Two consecutive price bars above the MAH constitutes a new uptrend and a change from an existing down trend.

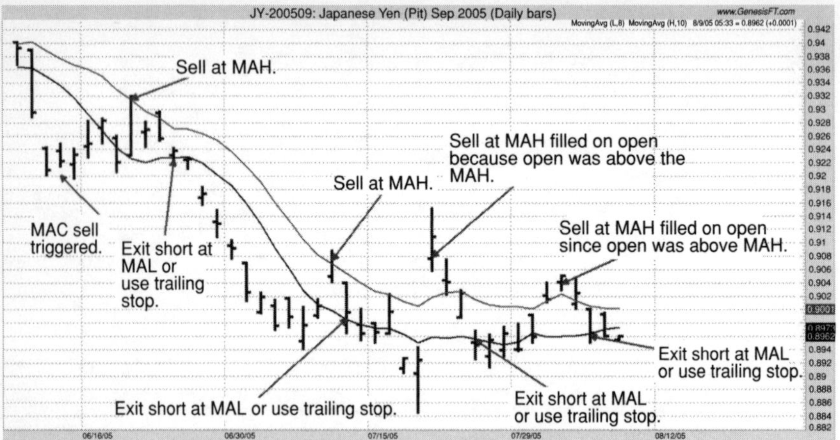

FIGURE 11.1 Short-term swing trading with the MAC.
Source: Courtesy of www.GenesisFT.com.

- Two consecutive price bars below the MAL constitutes a new downtrend and a change from an existing uptrend.
- You can buy or sell or reverse positions accordingly, however, I strongly suggest using another trend change indicator to confirm trend change signals based on the MAC in order to increase accuracy. The AD/MA indicator (to be discussed later in this lesson) can be used for this purpose.
- You have achieved your initial profit target—the MAL.
- The stop-loss on this trade is twice the width of the channel as measured on the day that the trade is entered or a reversing MAC signal.

See Figures 11.1 and 11.2 for examples.

MAC APPLICATION USING THE FIVE CONSECUTIVE BAR PATTERN

The last lesson indicated that the more consecutive bars either above or below the MAC as part of a new signal, the greater the odds of a large move. This method uses five consecutive bars as a trigger for a specific method. The rules are as follows:

- When a new MAC buy signal occurs with five consecutive bars above the MAH, buy on the open of trading the sixth bar. The profit target is the range of the five bars. Take profit at the profit target or take partial profit and trail a stop.

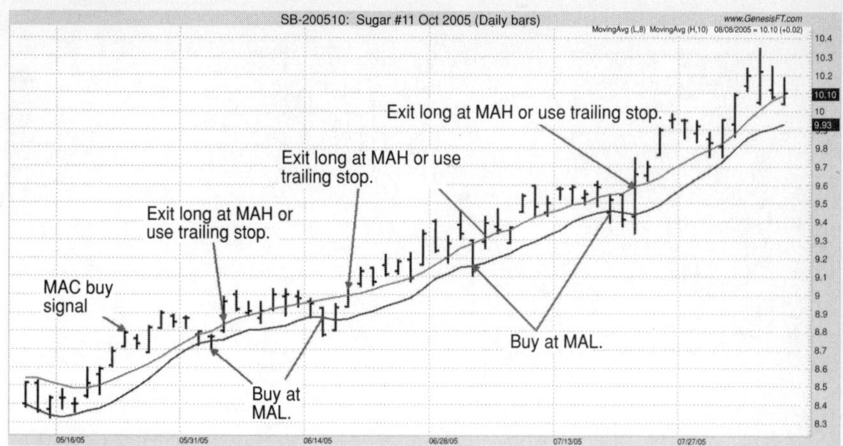

FIGURE 11.2 Short-term swing trading with the MAC.
Source: Courtesy of www.GenesisFT.com.

- When a new MAC sell signal occurs with five consecutive bars below the MAL, then sell on the open of trading the sixth bar. The profit target is the range of the five bars. Take profit at the profit target or take partial profit and trail a stop.
- Initial stop-loss is the range of the five bars or a reversing signal.

Figures 11.3 and 11.4 show examples of this method.

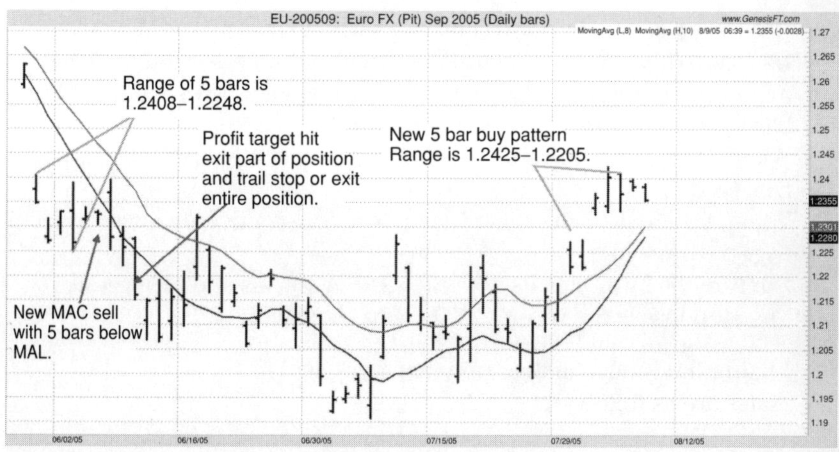

FIGURE 11.3 Example of the five-bar MAC pattern.
Source: Courtesy of www.GenesisFT.com.
Note: If you use a 57 period of MA of the AD you will tend to have fewer signals, but with somewhat higher accuracy.

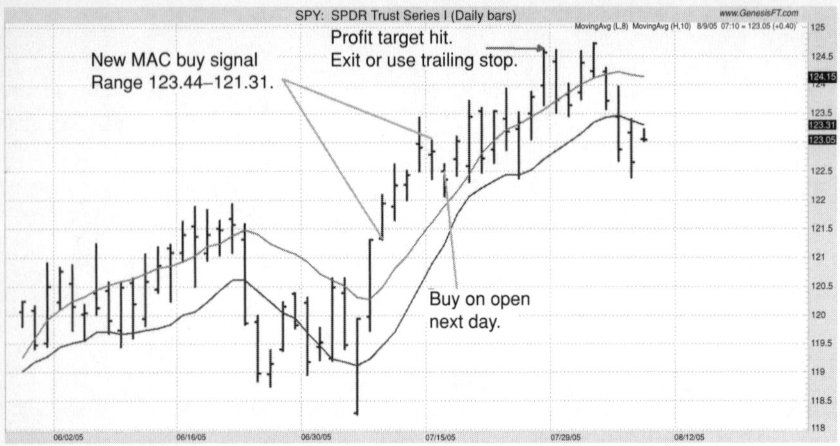

FIGURE 11.4 Another example of the five-bar MAC pattern.
Source: Courtesy of www.GenesisFT.com.

MAC APPLICATION USING THE ACCUMULATION-DISTRIBUTION MA

The last application of the MAC is to use the basic MAC buy and sell signals with the *Williams accumulation distribution/moving average indicator (AD/MA)*. Here are the rules of application followed by several examples:

- Use the basic two-bar MAC buy and sell signals with the AD/MA.
- Use the Williams accumulation distribution indicator and a 28-period moving average of the AD. Note that you will not be using the volume-based accumulation-distribution indicator.
- When AD moves above its MA for two consecutive postings, a buy is triggered.
- When AD moves below its MA for two consecutive postings, a sell is triggered.
- Confirm the MAC signals with the AD/MA signals and vice versa.
- The stop-loss is the reverse of the current signal.

Figures 11.5 and 11.6 illustrate this approach.

SUMMARY

The MAC is a highly versatile method that has a variety of applications as discussed in this lesson. These applications are not mutually exclusive. By

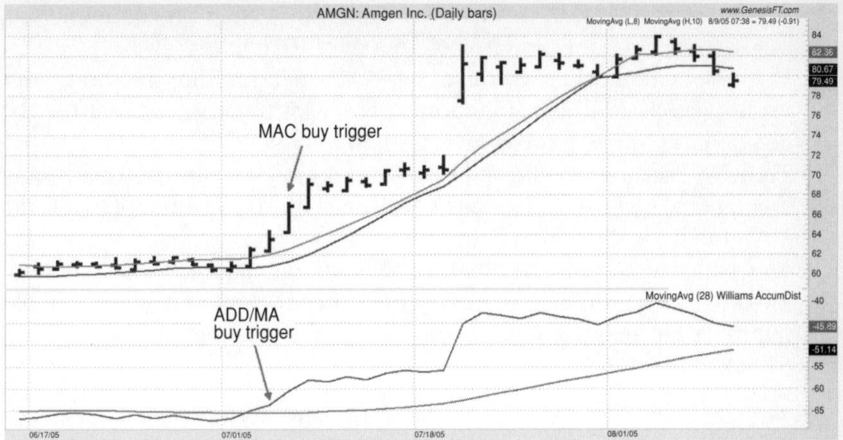

FIGURE 11.5 How the AD/MA signals work.
Source: Courtesy of www.GenesisFT.com.

this I mean that you can apply all of these at the same time. The way in which you do so is up to you. Here are some important tips for using the MAC successfully:

- Use the MAC in active markets only. If a market is thinly traded, then the price bars will be small and the accuracy of the MAC poor. If you use the daily price chart for futures, then use the lead month or active month.

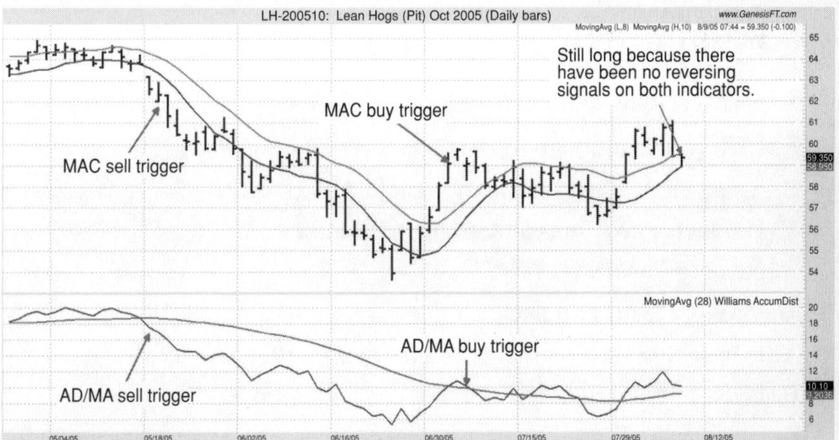

FIGURE 11.6 Another example of how the AD/MA signals work.
Source: Courtesy of www.GenesisFT.com.

- If you use the MAC in the intraday time frame, then I recommend you not use the MAC for time frames less than 10 minutes.
- Remember that when you use the MAC swing trading method, your profits are limited as a function of the width of the channel for the given market in which you are trading.
- The MAC methods require experience and should not be used in a totally mechanical fashion. Get some experience before you attempt to use the MAC methods described here.
- You can use the MAC with the Williams accumulation-distribution/moving average indicator as described in this lesson if you are looking for a more systematic methodology. You can use either a 28 or a 57 MA of the AD.

Now that you have learned the different methods in which you can use the MAC, it is time to practice again. Spend a good amount of time with the MAC.

REVIEW

Congratulations! You have now completed the MAC method. In this lesson, you learned the additional applications of the MAC and their specific rules.

In Lesson 12, we look at a specific price pattern designed to help short-term traders achieve consistency and profitability.

LESSON 11 QUIZ

Instructions: Circle the correct answers.

1. The MAC can be combined with the AD/MA to:

A. Give you a complete trading method that improves accuracy.

B. Give you detailed information on insider trading.

C. Produce a good spread trading method.

D. None of the above.

2. The five-bar MAC pattern:

A. Is based on the commercials and their market activity.

B. Is the method of choice for spreads and options.

C. Gives a buy signal when there are five consecutive bars above the MAH as part of a new buy trigger.

D. Is one of the few methods that does not have a profit target.

3. When using the MAC as a swing method:

   A. You buy at the MAH in an uptrend and wait for a breakout.

   B. You only use the MAC in sideways markets.

   C. You buy at the MAL in an uptrend and take profits at the MAH.

   D. None of the above.

4. The basic MAC buy and sell signals are:

   A. 88 percent accurate.

   B. Only used on weekly charts.

   C. A valuable method when used with a confirming indicator.

   D. All of the above.

5. Select all items that are true:

   A. The MAC has several specific applications.

   B. The MAC can give you a very specific idea of trend.

   C. The MAC can help you spot changes in trend.

   D. The MAC should not be used in thin markets.

6. The initial profit target for an MAC buy swing trade is:

   A. 0 percent of the range of the last 21 trading sessions.

   B. The high of the last five bars.

   C. The MAC high of the last 27 bars.

   D. The MAH.

7. The five-bar MAC pattern profit target is:

   A. The range of the five bars.

   B. The weighted moving average of the five-bar close.

   C. The Fibonacci ratio of the angle of ascent.

   D. The AD/MA.

8. The stop-loss for the five-bar MAC pattern is:

   A. The same as the profit target.

   B. The AD/MA low.

   C. The MAL.

   D. All of the above.

LESSON 12, DAY 12

Three Powerful Price Patterns: Part I

Lesson 11 finalized my discussion of the moving average channel (MAC). Lessons 12 and 13 show you three specific price patterns in the stock and commodity markets. Each is effective in its own right.

These are relatively short-term indicators; however; their implementation can also lead to longer-term opportunities. While some of these patterns may seem familiar to you, please note that I do not necessarily implement them the way most traders do. So please note well the differences and above all observe that these methods *all* use the setup, trigger, and follow-through method discussed in previous lessons.

I also want to reiterate that the STF structure is the most important procedure that you can follow in all stock and futures trading (as well as most other forms of speculation and investing). This lesson is considerably more detailed than what you have seen in the lessons so far. You need to read it over a few times to get it straight. Note that, although these are primarily day trades, they do not require you to watch the markets all day long.

If you do not have an interest in day trading then you can skip this chapter. Nevertheless, I think that the concept of the gap will be helpful to you because gap days tend to mark important turning points above and beyond the day that they occur.

PATTERN 1: THE GAP TRADE

The *gap trade* (GT) is one of the simplest short-term methods in existence. Paradoxically, it is also one of the most misunderstood methods. Here are the rules of application:

- Use day-session daily-price data only (i.e., pit session).
- If a market opens below the low of the previous day, the market has set up a gap buy trade.
- If a market opens above the high of the previous day, the market has set up a gap sell trade.
- After a *gap trade buy* setup (GTB), a trigger occurs when and if the market goes back up through the low of the previous day by a certain number of ticks.
- After a *gap trade sell setup* (GTS), a trigger occurs when and if the market goes back down through the high of the previous day by a certain number of ticks.
- There are three follow-through methods as follows:
  - Exit on stop-loss (to be discussed).
  - Exit on close of day win or lose if not stopped out.
  - Exit on *first profitable opening* (FPO).

These three follow-through methods will be discussed later in this lesson.

THE IMPORTANCE OF GAP DAYS

Gap days are very important because they often have the following common characteristics:

- Many major tops and bottoms occur on gap days.
- The trading range on gap days tends to be large.
- Gap days often occur as a result of news.
- Gap days provide very reliable day trading and short-term trading opportunities.
- Gap days tend to be highly emotional.
- The close on a gap day tends to be near the extreme of the day.
- The opening on a gap day tends to be near the extreme of the day.
- Trading volume tends to be large on gap days.

Figures 12.1 and 12.2 show visual schematics of gap buy and sell trades.

Figure 12.3 shows how the gap buy and sell signals look on an S&P futures chart.

FOLLOW-THROUGH ON GAP TRADES

As noted earlier, there are three aspects to the gap trade method. We have already examined them in general terms. Now let us get specific.

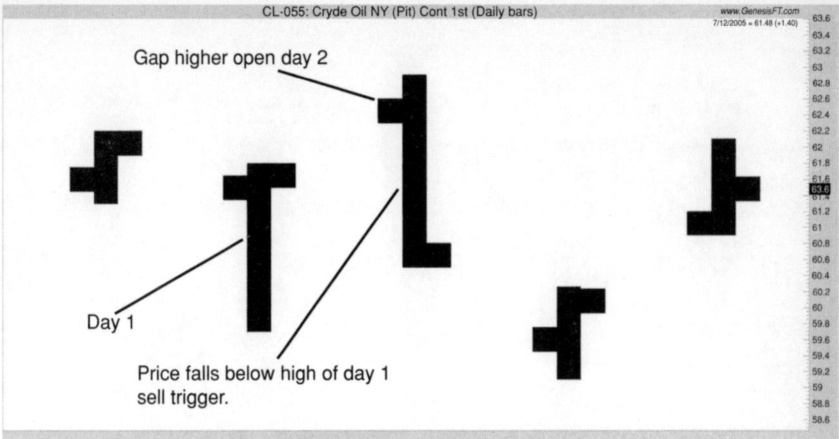

FIGURE 12.1 Schematic of ideal GTS that triggered.
Source: Courtesy of www.GenesisFT.com.

- If a market opens on a gap above the high of the previous day by more than a certain amount (i.e., the penetration amount), then place an order to go short a given amount below the high of the last day (see below for amount).
- The amount that a market opens above the high of the last day is called *gap size* (GS).

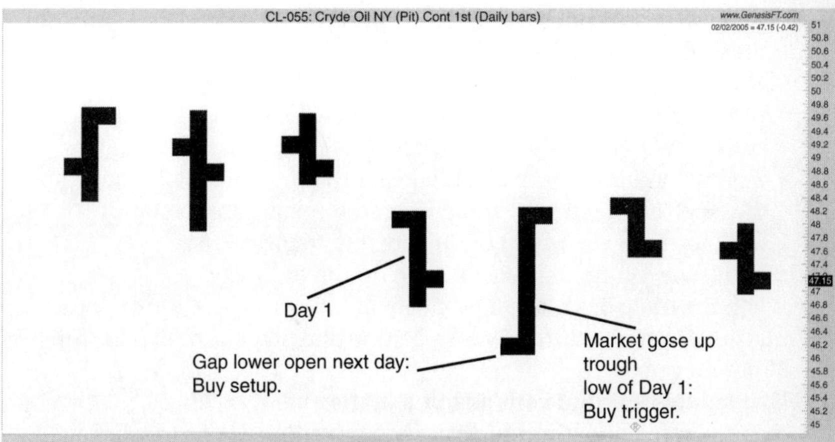

FIGURE 12.2 Schematic of ideal GTB that triggered.
Source: Courtesy of www.GenesisFT.com.

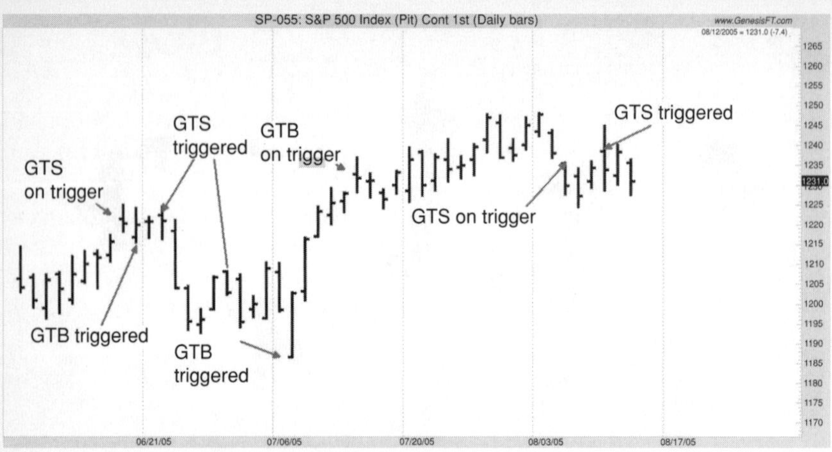

FIGURE 12.3 Various gap setups and triggers.
Source: Courtesy of www.GenesisFT.com.

- The amount that a market must drop back below the high of the last day is called the *penetration amount* (PA).
- In futures markets, the GS should be at least two ticks.
- In stocks the GS should be at least 5 percent of the previous daily trading range. For example, if a stock had a high of 35 and a low of 33 on the previous day, then the range is 2.00 and 5 percent of a 2.00 range is 10 cents. Therefore, the size of the opening of the next day should be at least 35.10 for a gap up open or a 32.90 for a gap down open.
- In futures the PA should be at least two ticks.
- In stocks the PA should be at least 5 percent of the previous daily range as described in this list.
- Once a trade has triggered, you can do the following:
  - Use a dollar-risk stop. This is not the best stop-loss because it is not system related. It is, however, one way of limiting risk.
  - Use a stop-loss that is 25 percent of the previous daily range above the price at which your trade triggered (examples to come).
- Exit your trade at the end of the day if not stopped out.
- If you trade multiple positions then do the following:
- When the trade has made a profit equal to the range of the previous day take profit on one-third of your position and place a follow-up stop-loss at breakeven.
- Exit another third of your position at the end of the day.
- Exit the remaining third of your position either at the breakeven stop-loss or on the *first profitable opening* (FPO).

See the next section for explanation of FPO.

FIRST PROFITABLE OPENING EXIT RULE (FPO)

The exit strategy is one of the most important aspects of a short-term trade. I first learned about the FPO exit from the long time trader and internationally known newsletter writer, Larry Williams. FPO is a very simple strategy. It means exactly what it says—you exit your position the first time it opens at a profit compared to the price at which you entered. If you are short, then you exit the first time the market opens at any price lower than the price you got in. If you are long, then you get out the first time the market opens at any price higher than the price at which you entered.

SAMPLE GAP TRADES: START TO FINISH

Figure 12.4 and Figure 12.5 demonstrate two sample gap trades from start to finish, one in a futures and one in a stock contract, complete with annotations showing application of the rules stated above.

Notes:

A: *Gap higher open.* Trade triggered short sale as it fell back through the previous days high. Short @ 108.20 with an exit at end of day at 105.30 and an FPO the next day on remainder of position at 105.

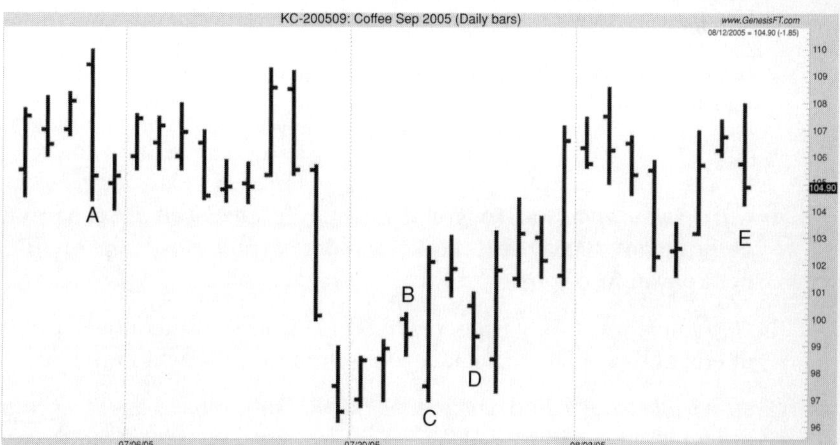

FIGURE 12.4 Gap trades in coffee futures.
Source: Courtesy of www.GenesisFT.com.

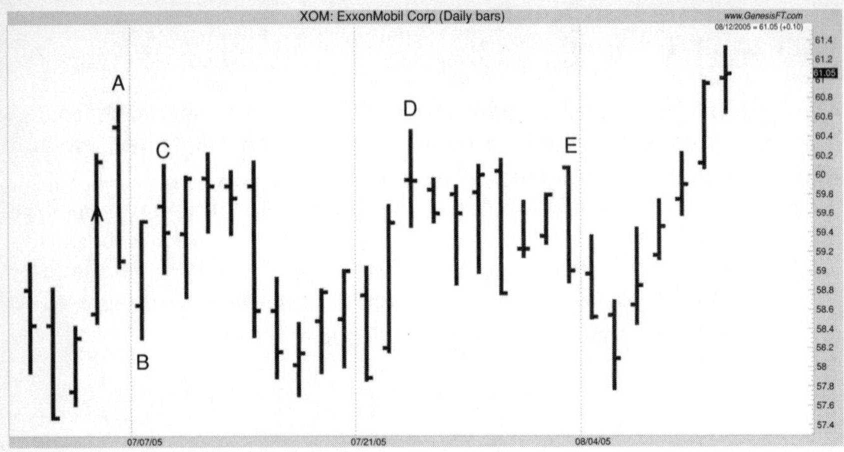

FIGURE 12.5 Gap trades in the stock of Exxon Mobil.
Source: Courtesy of www.GenesisFT.com.

B: *Gap higher open.* Trade triggered short sale as it fell back through the previous days high. Short at 99.05 out at a loss at the end of the day at 99.45.

C: *Gap lower open.* Trade triggered a buy as it penetrated back through the low of the previous day. Long @ 98.80 with an exit at end of day at 102.10. Another third of position out on FPO at 101.50.

D: *Gap lower open.* Long at 100.50. Out at a loss at the end of the day at 99.35.

E: *Gap lower open.* Buy triggered at 106.20. Out at end of the day at a loss at 104.90.

Notes:

A: *Gap higher open.* Sell triggered at 60.25. Trade closed out at a profit at the end of the day at 59.11. Remainder of trade closed out on FPO next day at 58.65.

B: *Gap lower open.* Buy triggered at 59.11. Trade closed out at a profit at end of day at 59.52. Balance closed out on FPO next day at 59.68.

C: *Gap higher open.* Sell triggered at 59.48. Trade closed out at a profit at end of day at 59.40. Balance of trade closed on FPO at 59.39.

D: *Gap higher open.* Short sell triggered at 59.60. Closed out at a loss at the end of the day at 59.94.

E: *Gap higher open.* Short sell triggered at 59.78. Trade closed out at the end of the day at 59.00. Balance of trade closed out on FPO at 58.97.

REVIEW

This lesson defined the gap trade with concise illustrations and definitions. Practical application of the method was stressed with specific examples. Please spend some time studying gap trades and applying your knowledge to the charts in the quiz that follows.

Please take a few minutes to answer the questions below. Note that this quiz will require more attention than previous quizzes. Take your time!

LESSON 12 QUIZ

Instructions: Mark the required points carefully according to your *best estimate*. You need not indicate the exact prices at which trades were triggered or closed out.

1. Mark the gap up and gap down days on the chart below and whether they triggered or not.

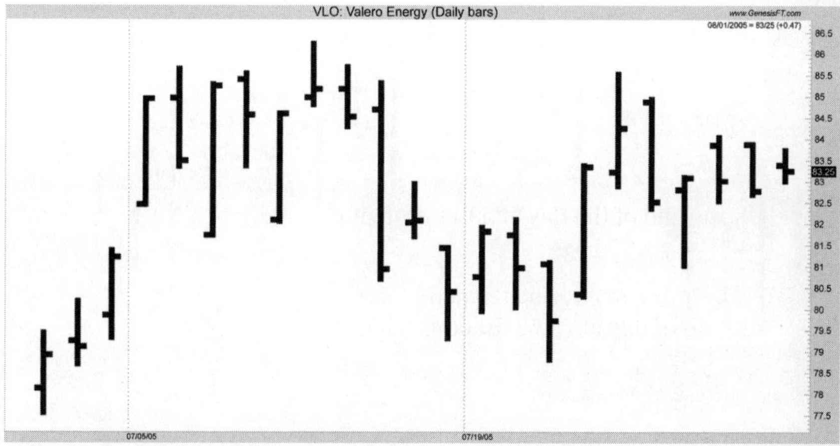

Source: Courtesy of www.GenesisFT.com.

2. Mark only the gap trades that triggered. Use your best estimate rather than calculating the exact points.

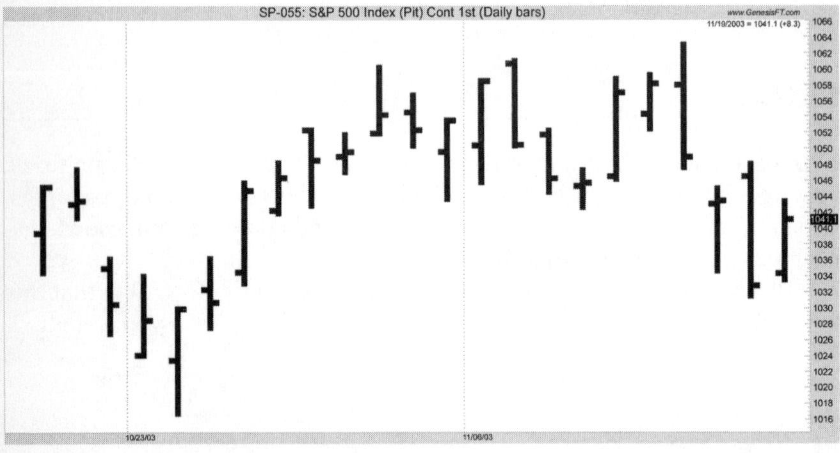

Source: Courtesy of www.GenesisFT.com.

3. Mark only the gap trades that triggered. Use your best estimate rather than calculating the exact points.

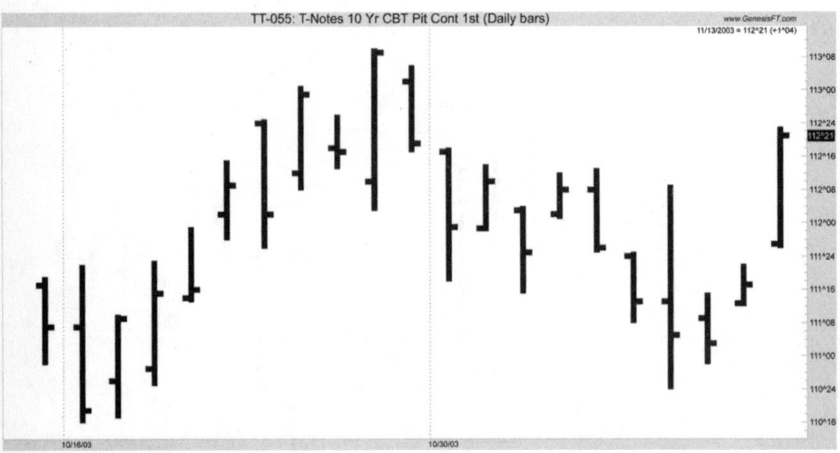

Source: Courtesy of www.GenesisFT.com.

4. Mark only the gap trades that triggered. Use your best estimate rather than calculating the exact points.

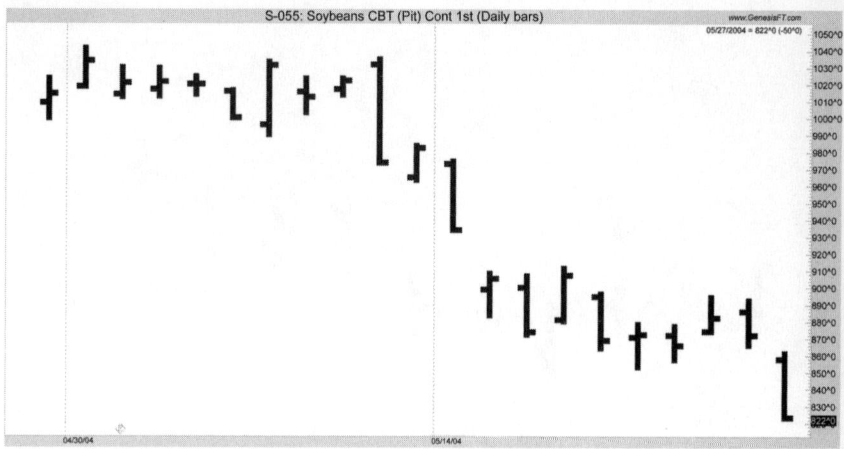

Source: Courtesy of www.GenesisFT.com.

5. Mark the gap trade that filled as well as the FPO point for this trade.

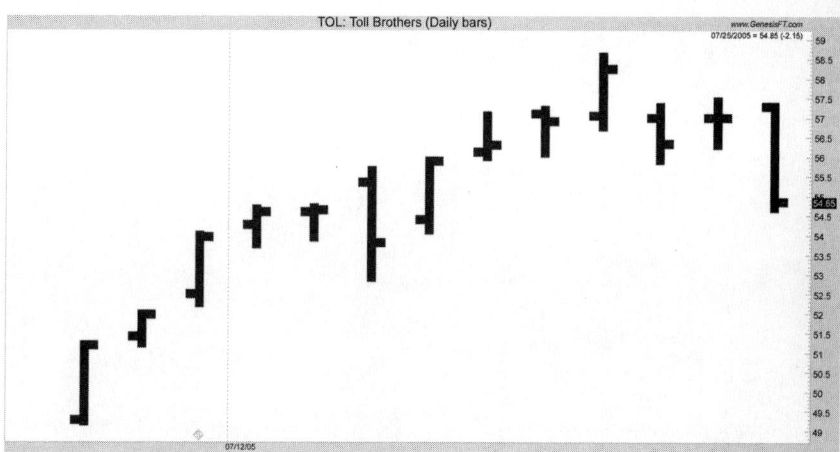

Source: Courtesy of www.GenesisFT.com.

6. Mark the gap trade that filled as well as the FPO point for this trade.

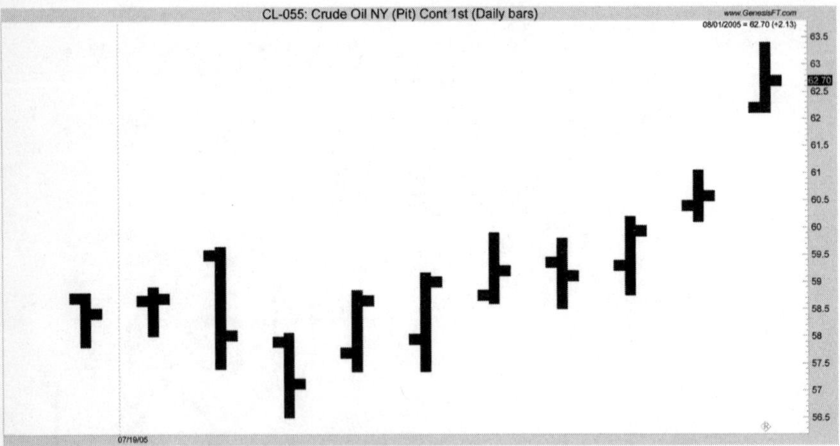

Source: Courtesy of www.GenesisFT.com.

LESSON 13, DAY 13

Three Powerful Price Patterns: Part II

Lesson 12 taught you the gap trade pattern. This pattern is also based on a gap but not a gap that is filled, rather on a gap that is not filled! To see what I mean by this last statement, read on.

PATTERN 2: THE TWO-DAY BREAKAWAY GAP

Some traders believe that a gap on a chart is significant. While I agree, I believe that most traders do not use chart gaps properly. To rectify that situation, let us look at gaps again. Before looking at a chart let's define the term "gap."

- A *gap up* occurs when a market opens above the high of the previous day and does not trade into the range of the previous day.
- A *gap down* occurs when a market opens below the low of the previous day and does not trade into the range of the previous day.
- Note that gaps can only be used on day session charts, not 24-hour charts.

Figure 13.1 shows examples of gap-up and gap-down patterns.

Most traders are familiar with gaps, of which there are several types. The gaps described above are all gaps, however, some are one-day gaps and others are two-day gaps. What is the difference? A one-day gap is a gap that

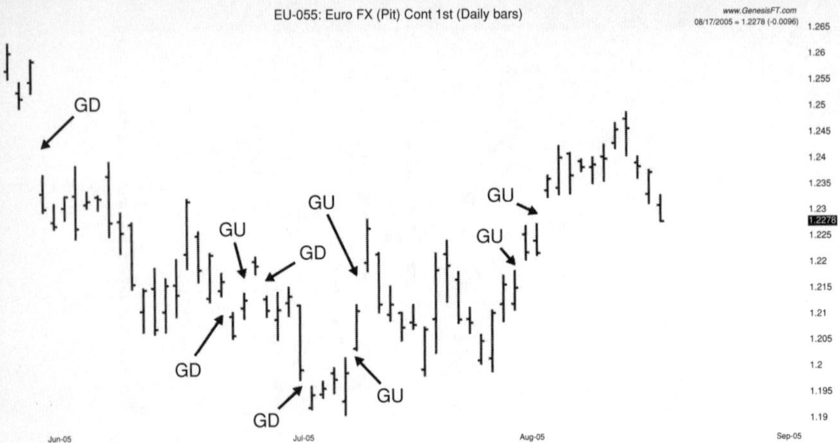

FIGURE 13.1 How gap-up and gap-down patterns look on a chart.
Source: Courtesy of www.GenesisFT.com.

develops over the course of one day. A two-day gap occurs over a two-day timeframe.

In terms of its reliability, the two-day gap results are significantly better than the one-day gap. Figure 13.2 shows a chart example of two-day gap-up and gap-down patterns.

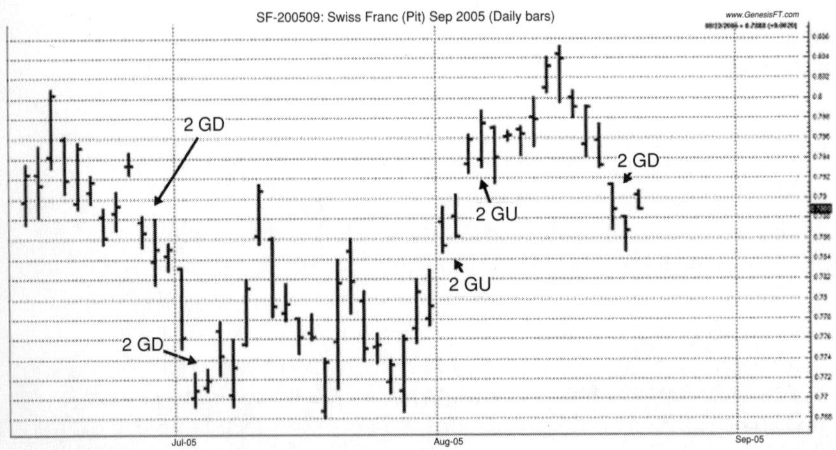

FIGURE 13.2 Two-day gap-up and gap-down patterns.
Source: Courtesy of www.GenesisFT.com.

SETUP AND TRIGGER

Now look at the setup and trigger for a two-day gap.

- Setup for a *buy* is a one-day gap up with this trigger: If the low of day 2 and the low of day 3 are higher than the high of day 1, then a two-day gap up has triggered on the close of day 3.
- Setup for a *sell* is a one-day gap down with this trigger: If the high of day 2 and the high of day 3 are lower than the low of day 1, then a two-day gap down has triggered on the close of day 3. Figure 13.3 illustrates the two-day gap-up and two-day gap-down setups and triggers.
- Entry for a long position on the two-day gap up is on the close of trading on the second day.
- Entry for a short position on the two-day gap down is on the close of trading on the second day.

Figure 13.4 illustrates the signals.

FOLLOW-THROUGH

- The profit target is the *range* of the two days that constitute the gap at which point you take profit on part of your position. Then you trail a stop at 75 percent on the balance of your position (i.e., locking in 75 percent of the profit).

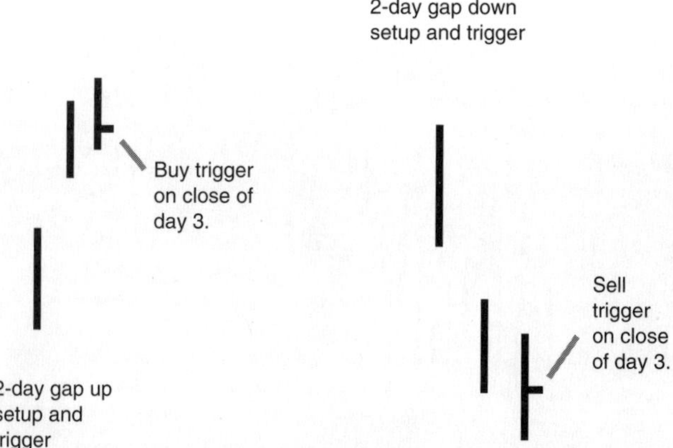

FIGURE 13.3 Two-day gap-up and gap-down setup and trigger.

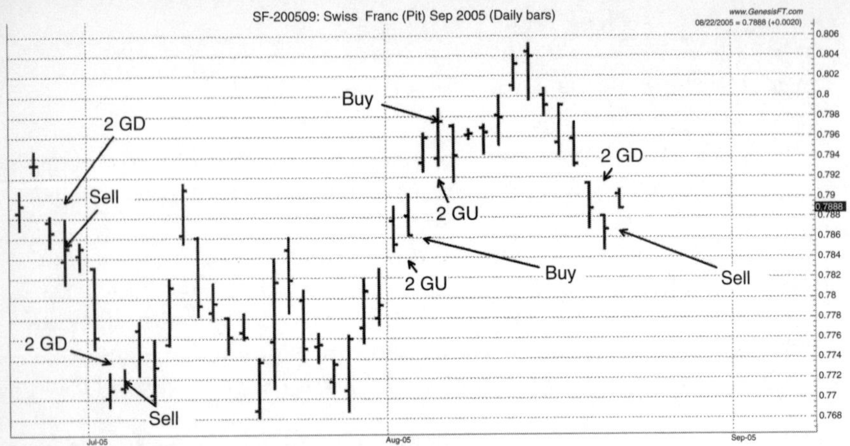

FIGURE 13.4 Two-day gap-up and gap-down setup and trigger.
Source: Courtesy of www.GenesisFT.com.

- The initial stop-loss is a close *above* the highest high of the two days of a sell gap or a close *below* the lowest low of the two days of the buy gap.
- Do not add to your position in the event of another signal in the same direction.

Figure 13.5 shows the gap signals as well as their entry and exit points.

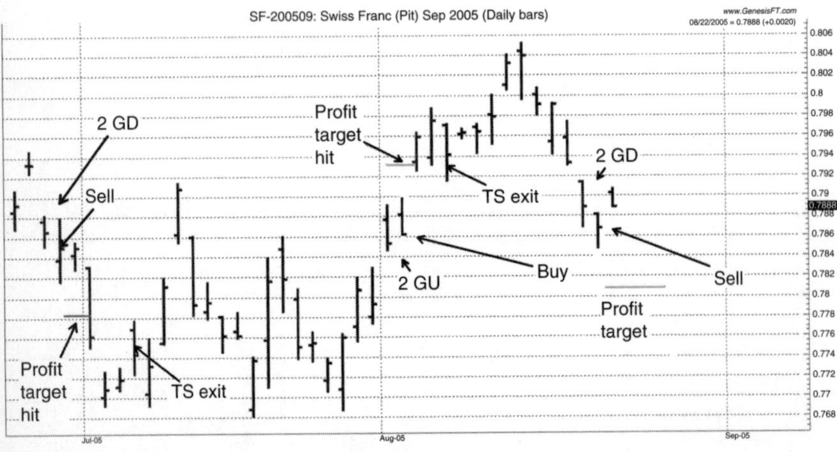

FIGURE 13.5 Gap signals entry and exit.
Source: Courtesy of www.GenesisFT.com.

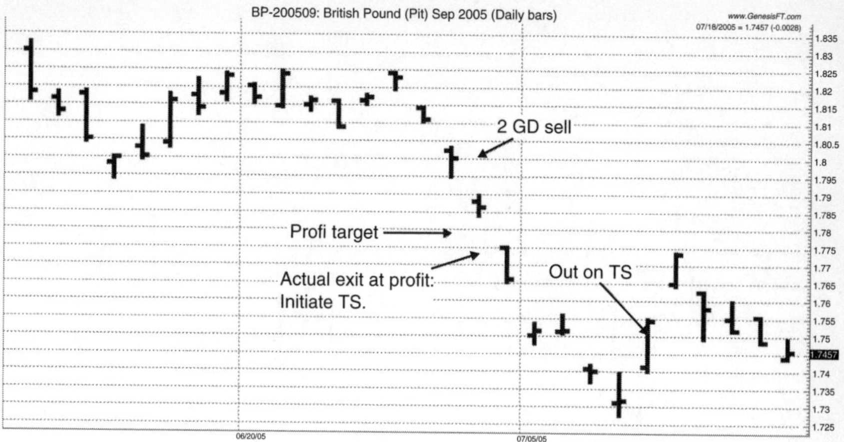

FIGURE 13.6 Another example of a gap trade.
Source: Courtesy of www.GenesisFT.com.

ANOTHER EXAMPLE

Figure 13.6 gives another example. Here the chart shows a two-day gap that was filled. First profit target was exceeded and a trailing stop was then implemented. Trade was stopped out as noted.

REVIEW

This lesson defined the two-day gap trade with concise illustrations and definitions. Practical application of the method was stressed with specific examples. Please spend some time studying two-day gap trades and applying your knowledge to the charts in the quiz that follows.

Please take a few minutes to answer the questions below. Note that this quiz will require more attention than previous quizzes. Take your time.

LESSON 13 QUIZ

Instructions: Please follow the indicated instructions carefully. Mark the signals, trades, and exits according to your *best estimate*. You need not indicate the exact prices at which trades were triggered or closed out unless you have access to a chart with exact prices.

For items 1 through 3, find and mark the two-day gap-up and gap-down triggers.

1.

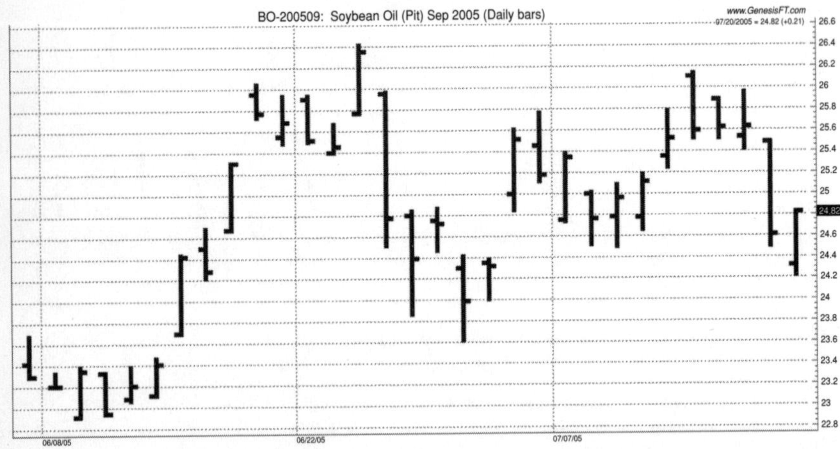

Source: Courtesy of www.GenesisFT.com.

2.

Source: Courtesy of www.GenesisFT.com.

3.

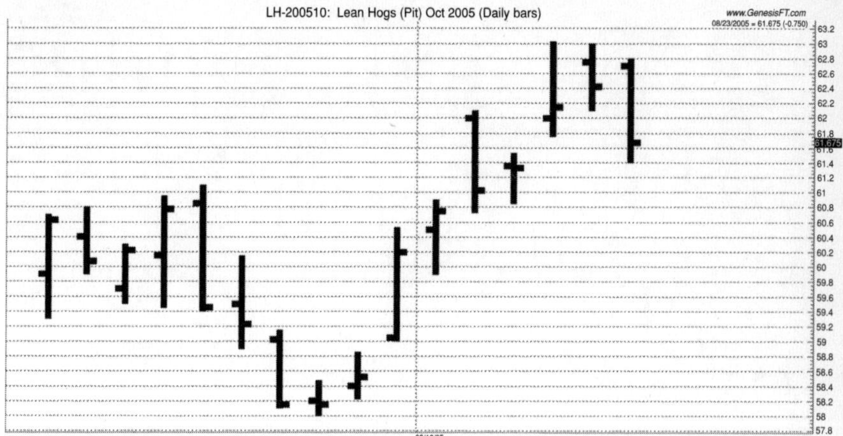

Source: Courtesy of www.GenesisFT.com.

For items 4 and 5, mark the two-day gap signal(s) and indicate the follow-through including profit target and trailing stop. Use your best estimate of the actual prices.

4.

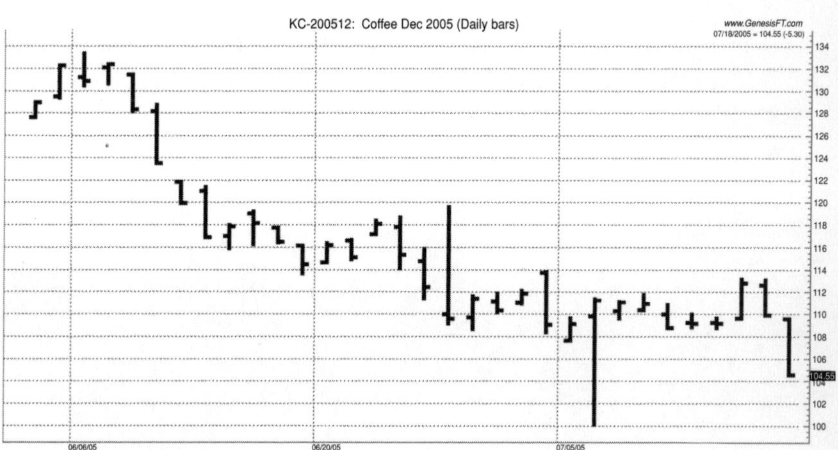

Source: Courtesy of www.GenesisFT.com.

5.

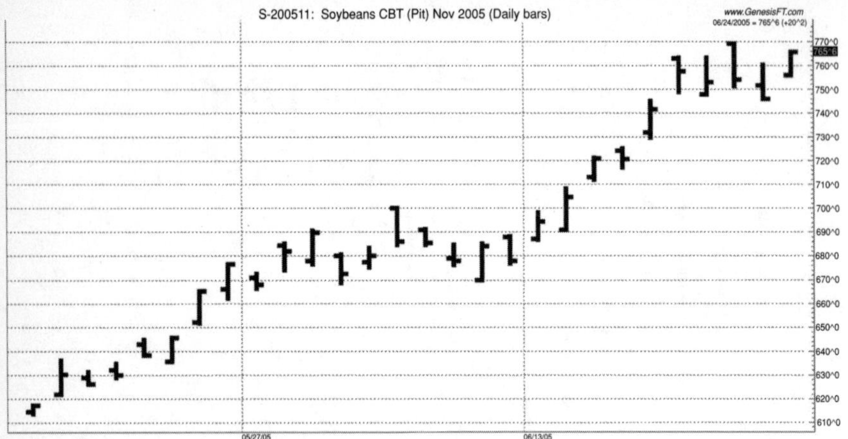

Source: Courtesy of www.GenesisFT.com.

LESSON 14, DAY 14

Three Powerful Price Patterns: Part III

Lesson 13 taught you the two-day gap trade pattern. The pattern you will learn in this lesson revisits a method that you already know from previous lessons.

The basis of this pattern is the moving average channel (MAC). I will assume that you have learned the basic signals. You may want to review the MAC lessons if you have forgotten some of the rules.

PATTERN 3: THE CMC

Humor me for a few minutes while I test your recollection of history. Do you remember the Cuban Missile Crisis? If so, you will recall that this was a time of considerable turmoil in relations between the Soviet Union, the United States, and Cuba. In fact, some historians now believe that we were closer to the brink of nuclear war than we have ever been. The crisis occurred in 1962 between October 18 and 29. It was a result of a naval blockade imposed by then President Kennedy to embargo all ships seeking to enter Cuban waters. The blockade was ordered in response to the shocking surveillance evidence that Cuba, with Soviet assistance, had installed nuclear-armed missiles, which were pointed at the United States.

Panic reigned supreme throughout the United States as the showdown unfolded. Many Americans retreated to their nuclear fallout shelters. Many others began building shelters, believing that war was imminent. The financial markets were also unhappy. The Dow Jones industrial average, which had already declined from a high of 734 in 1962 to a low of 524 in late June, began to drop again. The market dropped sharply on October 24.

While many investors panicked, savvy investors and traders were heavy buyers. They did so because they had evaluated the worst-case scenario. There were only several possibilities. First, the situation could stagnate and the stalemate could continue. This was unlikely due to the severity of the confrontation. Second, there could be a nuclear war. In this event, the United States would suffer severe causalities and damage. Depending on how serious the conflict would become, there might even be a complete cessation of stock trading. Finally, the third alternative was that the situation would be resolved peacefully, in which case stocks would soar. Prescient investors bought stocks because they felt that in the event of a nuclear war we would all be wiped out. There was every reason to buy stocks because the alternative was complete destruction. Those who bought on the bad news fared extremely well. From the late October low, stocks began a three-year bull market.

From this lesson of history, I coined the name of a pattern that occurs from time to time with the MAC. I call it the *Cuban Missile Crisis* (CMC) pattern. The rest of the lesson provides the details.

SETUP AND TRIGGER

The CMC pattern occurs *after* a market has triggered a MAC buy or sell signal. As you will recall, two consecutive price bars above the moving average (MA) of the high triggers a buy while two consecutive price bars below the MA of the low triggers a sell. Once there has been a trigger in a given direction, we consider the trend of the market to be consistent with the direction of the trigger.

What if a setup occurs that is opposite from the current trend? In other words, the market is in an uptrend and then you see one bar below the bottom of the channel. What's the worst-case scenario if you went *long* (that's right, long) at the end of that bar? The worst case would be one more consecutive bar below the channel that would trigger a sell, in which case you would exit the long and reverse to short.

However, what if the setup failed to trigger? What if the market went shooting back up? What you would have is an excellent position (at least for the short term). As an example, consider Figure 14.1.

As you can see from this example, the market shot right back up, rallying strongly and giving you a major profit. What if there had been a second bar below the channel low? The answer is simple—you would exit the trade or even reverse to the short side.

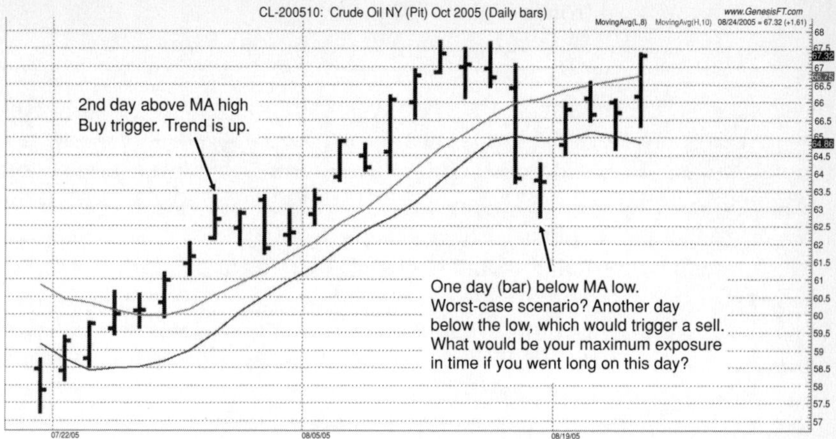

FIGURE 14.1 An example of the CMC pattern.
Source: Courtesy of www.GenesisFT.com.

Let us review the rules and then I will give you the follow-through for the CMC pattern, along with a few more chart examples.

- *Buy trigger.* After an MAC buy signal has occurred and the market is in an uptrend, buy on the close of trading of a bar that is completely below the moving average channel low.
- *Sell trigger.* After an MAC sell signal has occurred and the market is in a downtrend, sell on the close of trading of a bar that is completely above the moving average channel high.

FOLLOW-THROUGH

There are several types of follow-through for this method. Here are three types of follow-through for this method:

- Exit your position if the next day is completely below the channel low if you are long or completely above the channel high if you are short.
- Exit your entire position at the channel high MA if you are long or the channel low MA if you are short.
- Exit part of your position at the channel high MA if you are long or at the channel low MA if you are short and trail a stop-loss that locks in 75 percent of your maximum profit.

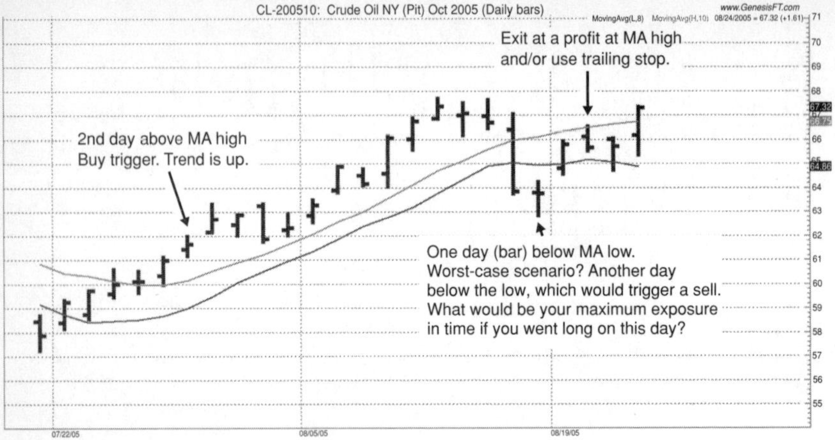

FIGURE 14.2 Another CMC signal.
Source: Courtesy of www.GenesisFT.com.

Use this method *only* during the most active portion of a futures contract (usually the last three months prior to first notice day) or in actively traded stocks.

EXAMPLES

Figures 14.2 through 14.5 show examples in stocks and commodities. The chart labels in the figures provide explanatory notes.

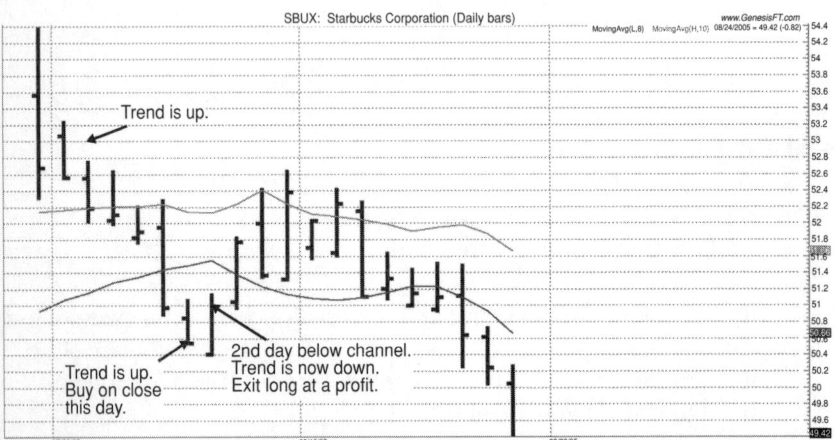

FIGURE 14.3 A CMC signal that failed but still produced a small profit.
Source: Courtesy of www.GenesisFT.com.

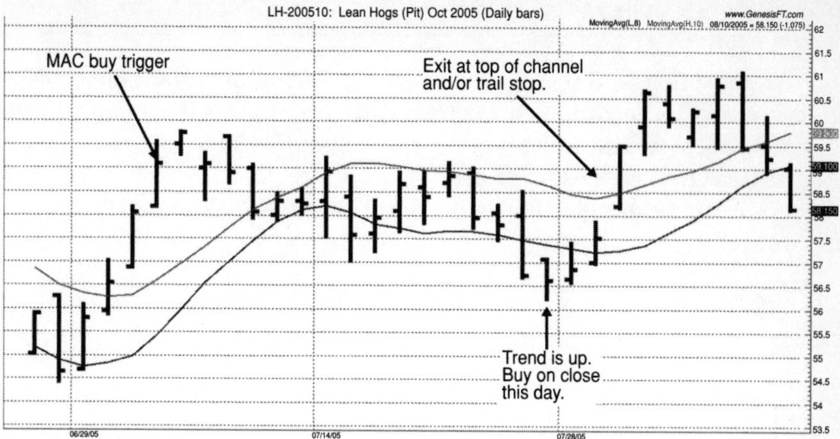

FIGURE 14.4 A CMC signal in lean hog futures.
Source: Courtesy of www.GenesisFT.com.

REVIEW

This lesson defined the CMC pattern with concise specific examples and definitions. Practical application of the method was stressed with specific examples. Spend some time studying CMC examples and applying your knowledge to the charts in the quiz that follows.

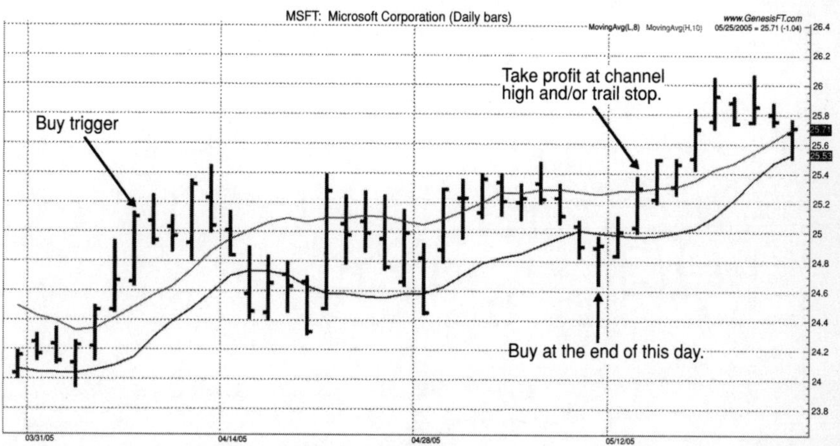

FIGURE 14.5 A CMC signal in Microsoft (MSFT).
Source: Courtesy of www.GenesisFT.com.

LESSON 14 QUIZ

Instructions: Follow the indicated instructions carefully. Mark the signals, trades, and exits according to your *best estimate.* You need not indicate the exact prices at which trades were triggered or closed out unless you have access to a chart with exact prices.

For items 1 through 5 find and mark the CMC signals and exits.

1.

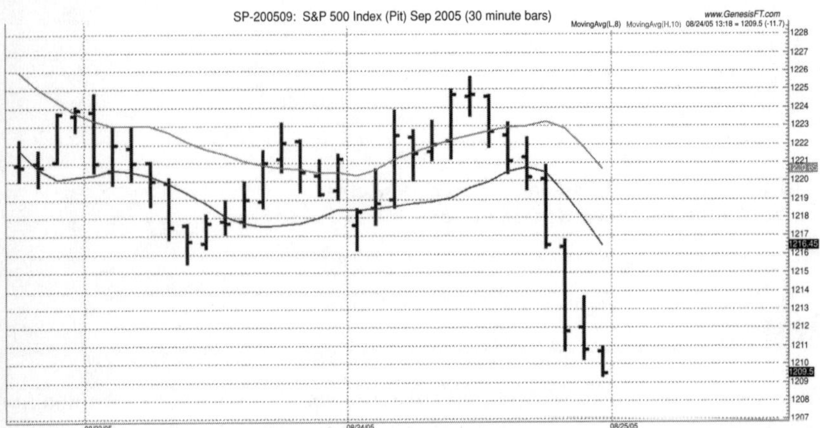

Source: Courtesy of www.GenesisFT.com.

2. There are four triggers here. Mark them and their outcome.

Source: Courtesy of www.GenesisFT.com.

3. There are two triggers on this chart. Find and mark them and mark their follow-through.

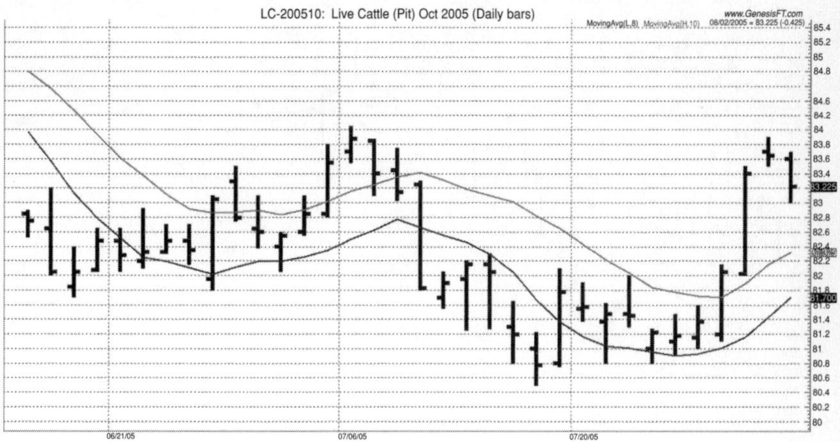

Source: Courtesy of www.GenesisFT.com.

4.

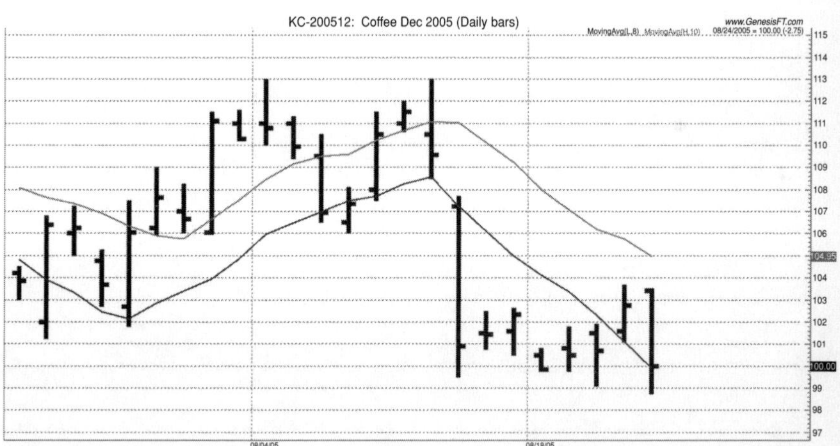

Source: Courtesy of www.GenesisFT.com.

5.

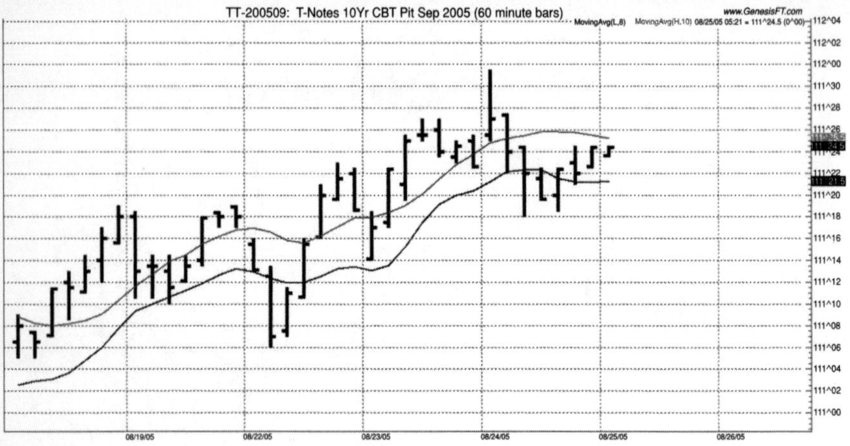

Source: Courtesy of www.GenesisFT.com.

LESSON 15, DAY 15

The Eight-Bar Open/Close Pattern and How to Use It

The third pattern in this series is the *eight-bar open/close moving average pattern.* It is a simple pattern that is based on the relationship between the opening and closing price of a price bar. Typically, market lows are preceded by a period of accumulation while market highs are often preceded by a period of distribution. One way to determine pending price tops or bottoms is to monitor the relationship between the opening and closing price of a market over a given period of time. If the close of a given price bar is higher than the open of a given price bar for a given period of time, then a low is likely. If the close of a given price bar is lower than the open of a given price bar a given period of time, then a high is likely.

The best way I have found to monitor this pattern is by using an eight-bar moving average of opening prices versus an eight-bar moving average of closing prices. Those who have attended my seminars and my former one-on-one mentoring students will remember the five-bar open/close indicator that I developed many years ago.

Since then I have used the method considerably, during which time I have refined it to the eight open/close pattern with a variety of follow-through approaches. Note that this method is *not* totally mechanical or objective. I offer it to you because it is a very effective method for spotting short-term price trend swings in active and trending markets.

Figure 15.1 is one example of the eight open/close pattern. As you can see, although it is a lagging indicator, it is fairly good at spotting trends. The three keys to effective use are:

1. The ability to trail a stop.
2. The ability to filter out small or minor crossovers that only last a day or two. One of these is illustrated in the noted section on the chart represented in Figure 15.1. In this case, the crossover lasted only one day. The way to deal with such situations is by requiring the crossover values to be more than a given amount (i.e., more than just one or two ticks in futures and more than a given percentage of the price of a stock).
3. Very often you will have a profit by the fifth day after the crossover. You can exit or trail a stop-loss.

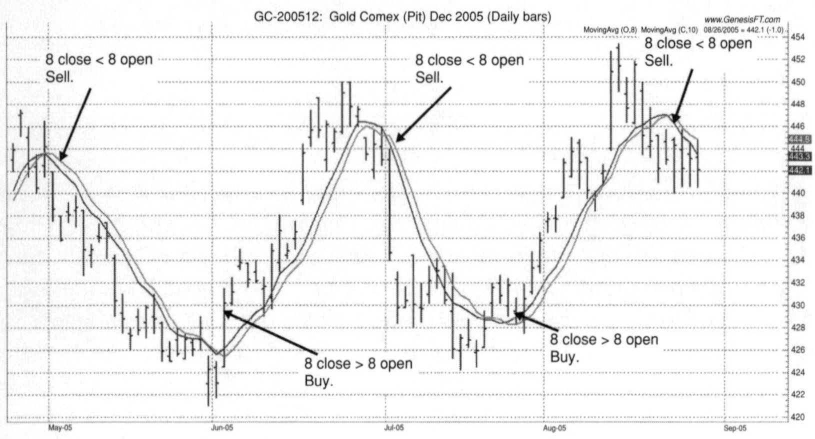

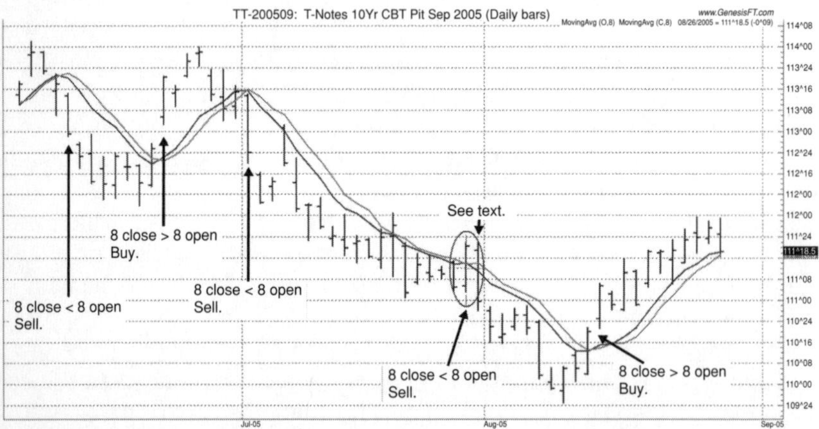

FIGURE 15.1 An illustration of the eight open/close method.
Source: Courtesy of www.GenesisFT.com.

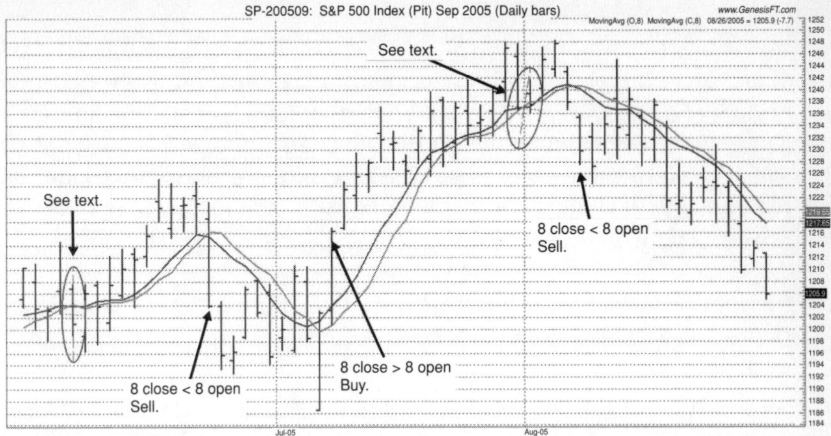

FIGURE 15.2 The eight open/close pattern in S&P futures.
Source: Courtesy of www.GenesisFT.com.

Figure 15.2 gives another example of this pattern. Here is a chart of S&P showing the eight open/close pattern. Note that there are two potential spots (labeled See Text) where the method reversed and then reversed back again. My suggestions in the next section help you minimize such instances.

SETUP AND TRIGGER

Note that the open/close indicator is *not* a trading system. It is merely a method for determining the relative strength or weakness of a market and/or the timing of a short-term trend change. It is best when used with another short-term indicator.

Now let's look at the setup and trigger for this pattern, after which I will show you a few suggested applications.

- A buy setup and trigger occur when the eight-bar moving average of the close goes above the eight-bar moving average of the open. Entry is on the close of the.the bar or on the open of the next bar.
- A sell setup and trigger occur when the eight-bar moving average of the close goes below the eight-bar moving average of the open. Entry is on the close of the bar or on the open of the next bar.

The method can be used in various time frames.

FOLLOW-THROUGH

There are several types of follow-through for this method. Note that this is a trading method as opposed to a trading system. By this I mean that a small amount of judgment is required as opposed to the purely mechanical procedures used in a trading system. There is more about this later on when I give you my suggestions for application. Here are four types of follow-through for this method:

1. Exit your position by reversing when the moving averages change their orientation. This is not recommended because you will give up too much profit.
2. Exit a portion of your position at a profit target that is equal to the range of the last eight bars prior to the trigger. See charts in Figures 15.3 and 15.4 for examples.
3. Exit your entire position as noted in item 2 and wait for the next signal. This method is not preferred since you will often miss the very large moves
4. Exit part or all of your position on the close of the fifth bar after entry if it is profitable.

Exit part of your position on the eighth bar after the last trigger and/or trail a stop on the balance of the position. However, if the trade shows a loss after the eighth bar, the odds are it will not be profitable and you may want to exit the entire position.

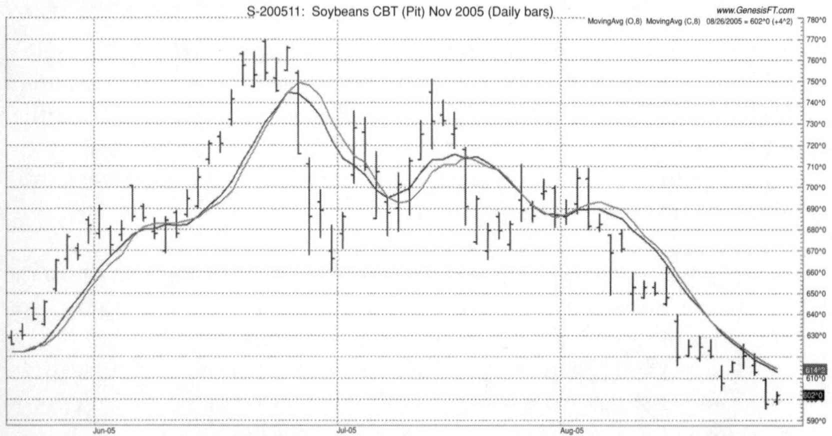

FIGURE 15.3 Trigger and follow-through on the eight open/close pattern.
Source: Courtesy of www.GenesisFT.com.

Because this method is *not* a mechanical trading system, but rather a method for determining short-term trend changes, you cannot use a rigid approach in trading with this method. In other words, this method is not totally objective compared to the methods that have been taught in previous lessons.

Figures 15.3 through 15.4 show the eight open/close pattern signals and a few examples of the applications suggested in this section.

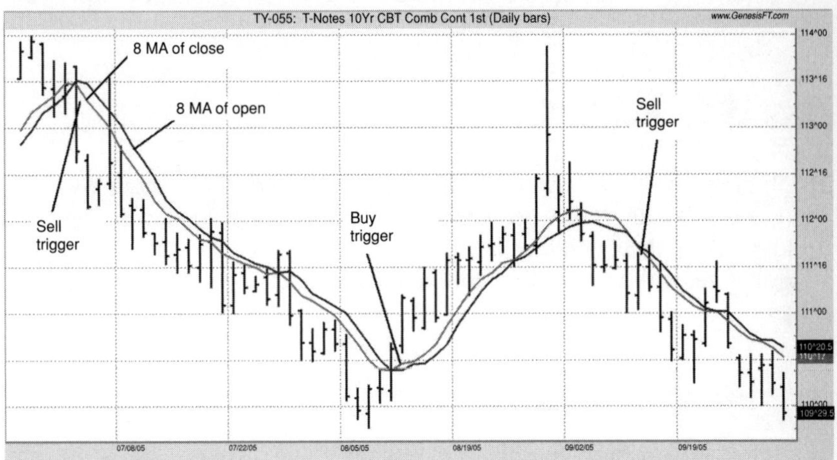

FIGURE 15.4 Trigger and follow-through on the eight open/close pattern. *Source:* Courtesy of www.GenesisFT.com.

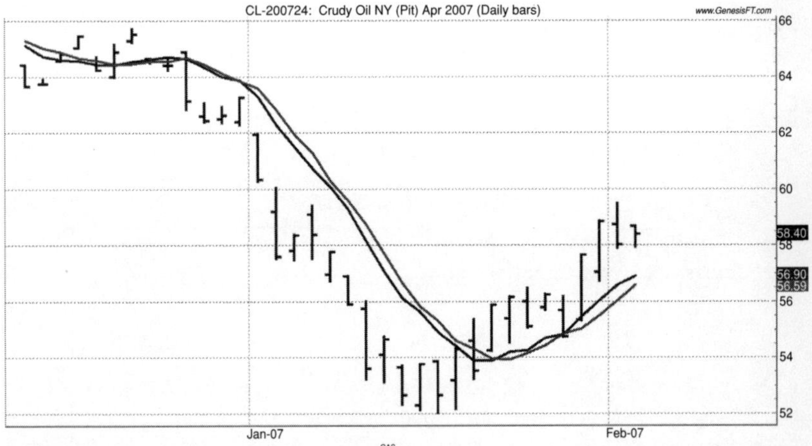

FIGURE 15.5 Trigger and follow-through on the eight open/close pattern. *Source:* Courtesy of www.GenesisFT.com.

REVIEW

This lesson taught you a simple method for determining and taking advantage of short-term trend changes using the eight open/close pattern. I emphasized that this pattern should *not* be considered a trading system but rather a method or indicator.

Please take a few minutes to answer the questions below. Note that this quiz requires more attention than some of the earlier quizzes. Take your time.

LESSON 15 QUIZ

Instructions: Mark the signals, trades, and exits according to your *best estimate*. You need not indicate the exact prices at which trades were triggered or closed out unless you have access to a chart with exact prices.

For items 1 through 3 find and mark the eight open/close buy and sell triggers.

1.

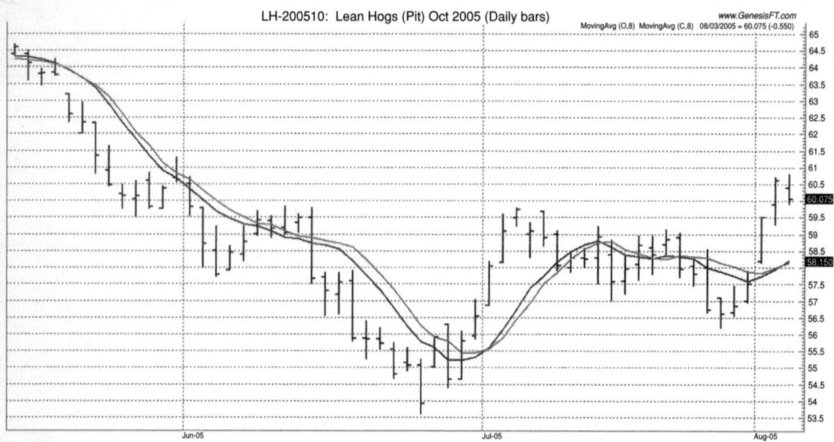

Source: Courtesy of www.GenesisFT.com.

2.

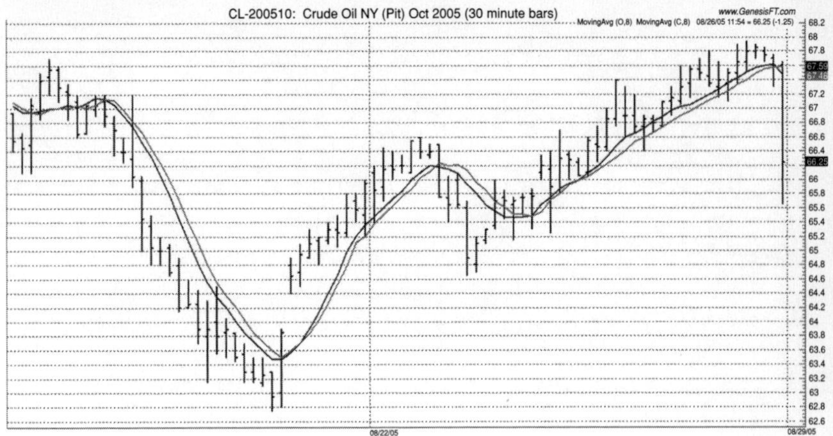

Source: Courtesy of www.GenesisFT.com.

3.

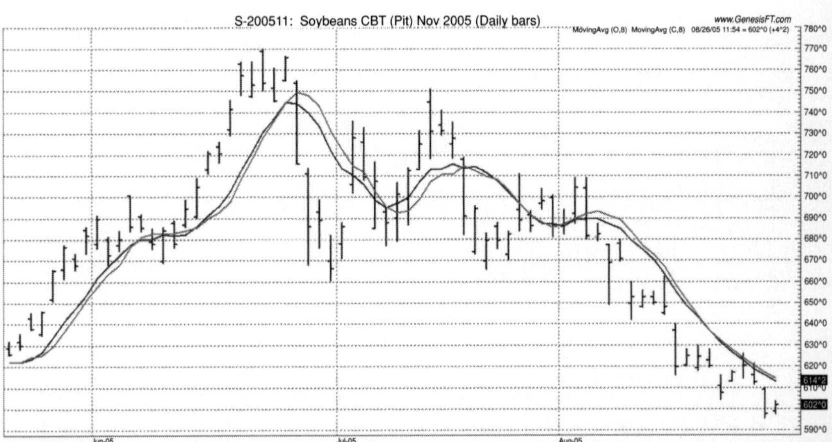

Source: Courtesy of www.GenesisFT.com.

For items 4 and 5 mark the eight open/close triggers and your ideas for follow-through per the suggestions given in this lesson using your best estimate of prices (unless you have access to actual prices).

4.

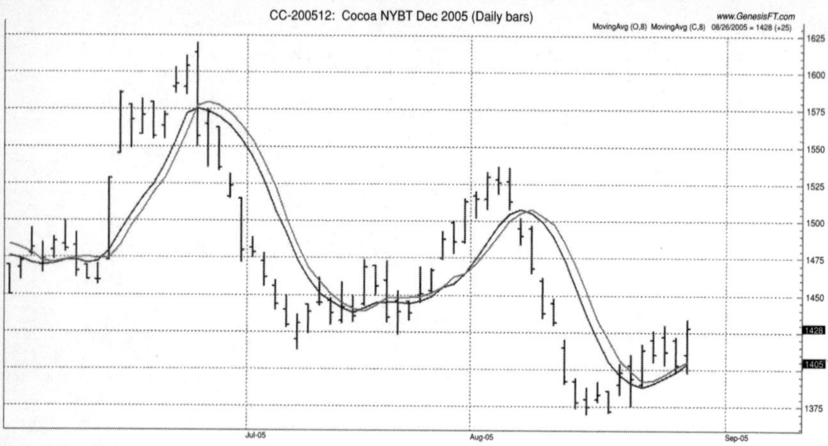

Source: Courtesy of www.GenesisFT.com.

5.

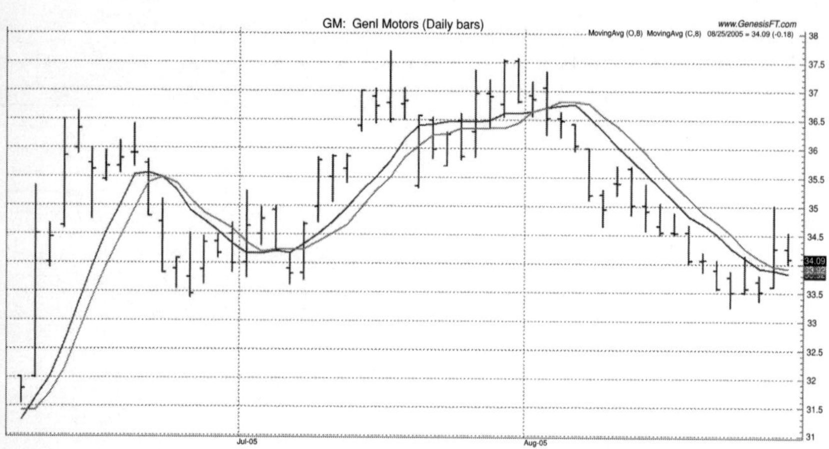

Source: Courtesy of www.GenesisFT.com.

LESSON 16, DAYS 16–17

Understanding and Using the Commitment of Traders Report: Part I

The *Commitment of Traders Report* (COT) is a very important tool for futures traders who are interested in spotting the big moves *before* they happen. This lesson examines the COT, its meaning, and my recommended applications. It should be noted that the COT report is not applicable to stock trading. If you only trade stocks you can skip this chapter.

Let us look at the information that is contained in the COT report.

The COT report is issued weekly by the *United States Commodity Futures Trading Commission* (CFTC). The report contains a detailed breakdown of the total number of long and short positions and changes in positions from the previous weekly report. Various market information and advisory services analyze the COT data shortly after it is released on the last business day of each week. You can see the report and read about its construction and history at the CFTC Web site at http://www.cftc.gov.

The best way to understand the COT report is by studying the position breakdown in three categories of traders: commercials, large speculators, and small speculators. The true value of this report cannot be ascertained unless you know what to look for.

Before we begin, I want to be clear that what you read in this lesson is my analysis, application, and understanding of the COT report. I say this because opinions about the meaning of the COT report vary from "useless" to "the Holy Grail." There is no lack of controversy about the COT. You may already have formed your own opinion based on what you have been told or what you have read. I ask you to rid yourself of any other opinions, at least for the duration of this lesson.

MARKET PARTICIPANTS

To fully understand the COT, you must understand the role and the goal of each group. Let us begin with the "small speculator" group. What exactly is a small speculator, and what do small speculators do? The answers are simple. Small speculators are exactly what the name implies. They are traders who trade small positions (one to three contracts) and/or who have a relatively small amount of money in their accounts. To put things simply, which is the best way to look at things, small speculators are generally considered to be poor traders (unless they have taken my course or seminars or worked one on one with me in my *Mentoring Program*). Prevailing opinion would have us believe that if we know what small traders are doing then we can make money by doing the opposite. I do *not* believe that this is true. If small traders always lost money, then they would not play the game.

Furthermore, looking at the correlation of small trader net long or short positions with price trends does not, in my view, support such a conclusion. The chart below is merely one example of what I mean. Note that the COT line plot at the bottom of the chart has a zero line. When the COT number is above the line it means that small traders are net long. When it is below the bottom line it means that small traders are net short. As the line rises, short positions are decreasing or long positions are increasing. As the line moves down, short positions are increasing or long positions are decreasing. See the notations in Figure 16.1.

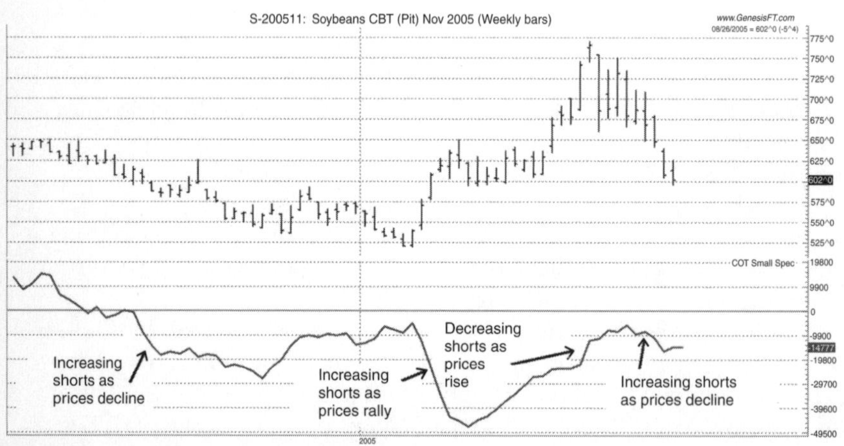

FIGURE 16.1 Small trader COT.
Source: Courtesy of www.GenesisFT.com.

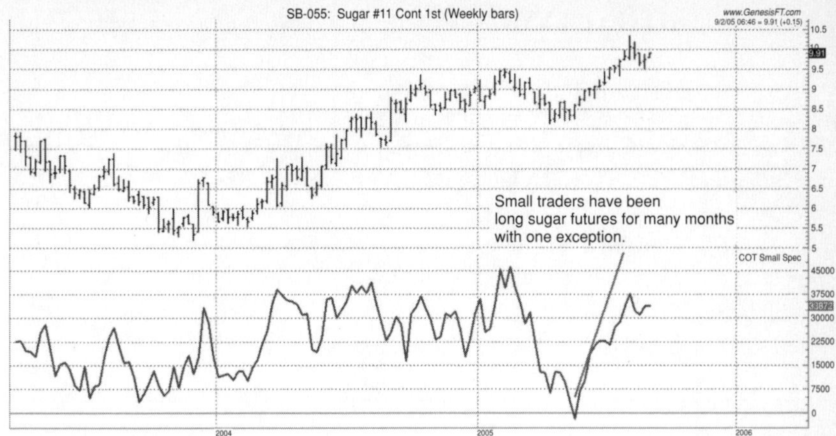

FIGURE 16.2 Large trader COT.
Source: Courtesy of www.GenesisFT.com.

As you can see from Figure 16.1, there was no consistent pattern other than the fact that small traders were net short soybeans for the duration of the bull market. In and of itself this information is, in my view, meaningless unless it is used with a clear and effective trigger. (Remember the STF model.) Another factor that limits the potential usefulness of the COT numbers is that by the time the report is available it is actually a week old. It cannot, therefore, be used for short-term timing.

Large speculators—such as the example shown in Figure 16.2—form the second category of statistical data in the COT report. It is generally believed that this group is more experienced and more correct than the small traders group.

Figure 16.3 shows an example of the typical relationship between COT large speculators data and prices. Large speculators are just what the name implies. These are individuals or businesses that either trade their own accounts or the accounts of other parties. Traders in this category tend to be trend followers.

So is the COT large speculator data of any value? I say no because it tells us what we already know and it does so about a week (if not more) after the fact. If a market is rising, then I can safely assume that large speculators will be long and vice versa in a falling market.

In reality, you could use virtually any trend-following tool and get the same result as if you followed the COT of large speculators—and you would get the information sooner.

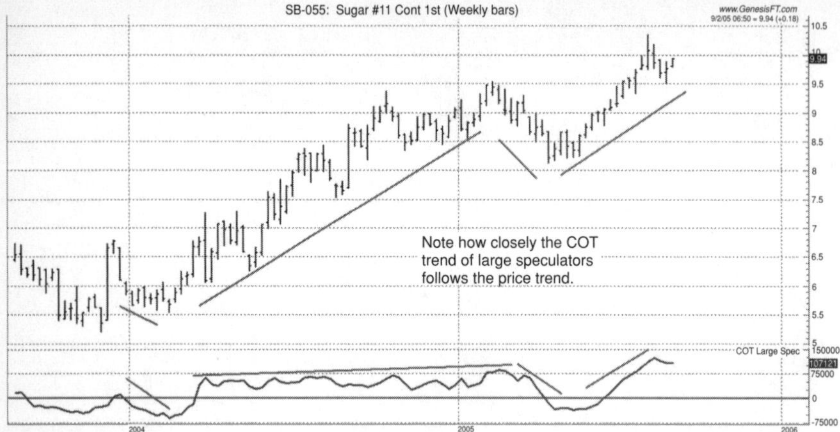

FIGURE 16.3 The close relationship between large speculator COT and price trends.
Source: Courtesy of www.GenesisFT.com.

COMMERCIALS

The third category of the COT report is *commercials*. Commercials have several functions. They are firms that either use the commodities (end users), or are producers of the product (mining companies, farmers, petroleum companies, meatpackers, ranchers, etc.). Commercials are, in my view, *not* speculators. They either use the stuff or they are intermediaries between the producers and the end users. While you may read a great deal of information about how to use the COT commercials data, I want to "cut to the chase" and tell you what I see and suggest:

- The normal job of commercials is to be hedged in the market. In other words, their COT data typically show as a minus number. This does NOT mean that they are all short the market. If a commercial firm buys corn from a farmer and then sells it in the futures market, I do not consider this to be a short position since they own the product. Still, however, a hedge position shows as a short position on the COT report. This is very misleading to people who do NOT know what the COT commercials data mean. This aspect of the COT data is not particularly helpful to me, with one exception (to be explained in the next lesson).
- When the COT commercials data show as a positive number, the odds favor a rally. Commercials need the product for their end users and they buy it in the futures markets. Because commercials can accumulate long

positions well in advance of a rally, a positive COT number does not mean that you should immediately go long a market. A trigger is still necessary. A positive COT commercials number is a leading indicator of a bull market. Frequently these bull moves can take a long time to develop.

- The best use of COT commercials data is for spotting major trends in prices before they begin.

Figure 16.4 illustrates what I mean. See my notations.

Figure 16.5 gives another example of the COT commercials and price.

The next issue is the trigger. How can we use a trigger with the COT commercials? This topic will be discussed in Lesson 17.

REVIEW

This lesson teaches you my method for spotting large bull markets by understanding the meaning of the COT report. I suggested not paying attention to the COT numbers for small traders and large traders. There are some ways in which these can be useful but I find that there are better methods. The goal in using COT commercials data is to spot coming bull moves before they begin.

Please take a few minutes to answer the questions below. Note that this lesson's quiz requires more attention than some quizzes due to the fact that

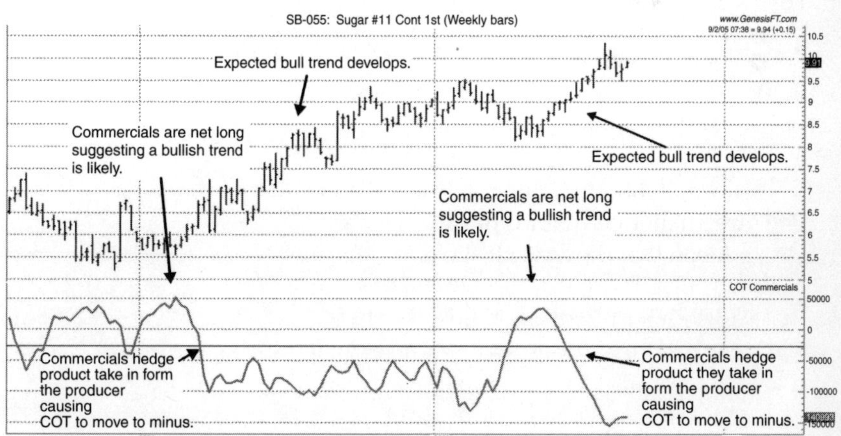

FIGURE 16.4 How commercials take positions in relation to price trends and anticipated price trends.
Source: Courtesy of www.GenesisFT.com.

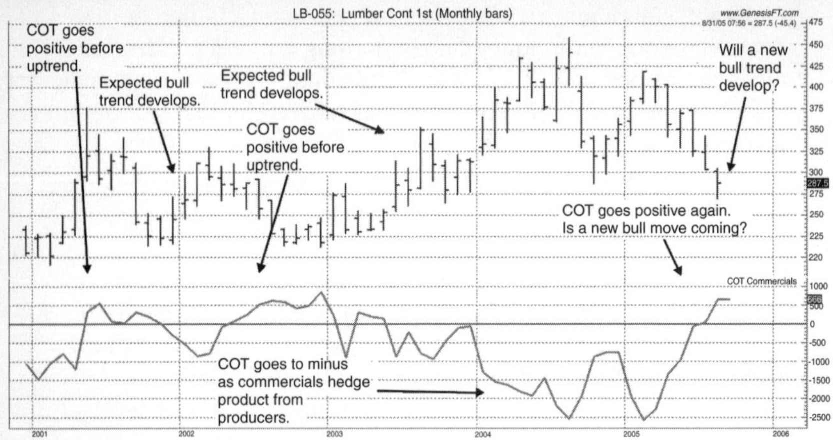

FIGURE 16.5 COT commercials and lumber price trends.
Source: Courtesy of www.GenesisFT.com.

a degree of judgment is required when answering the questions that involve chart interpretation. Take your time.

LESSON 16 QUIZ

Please circle the correct answer.

1. The weekly Commitment of Traders Report is:

   A. Best used for determining large moves in futures.
   B. Best used for finding longer term moves in futures.
   C. Issued by the commodity futures trading commission.
   D. All of the above.

2. The three major categories of COT data are:

   A. Winners, losers, and hedgers.
   B. Day traders, spreaders, and Forex traders.
   C. Cattle producers, soybean producers, and moving averages.
   D. Commercials, large speculators, and small speculators.

3. When commercials are showing as short on the COT data:

   A. They are really long.
   B. They are actually hedged.

C. They are not in the market.

D. They expect a big down move.

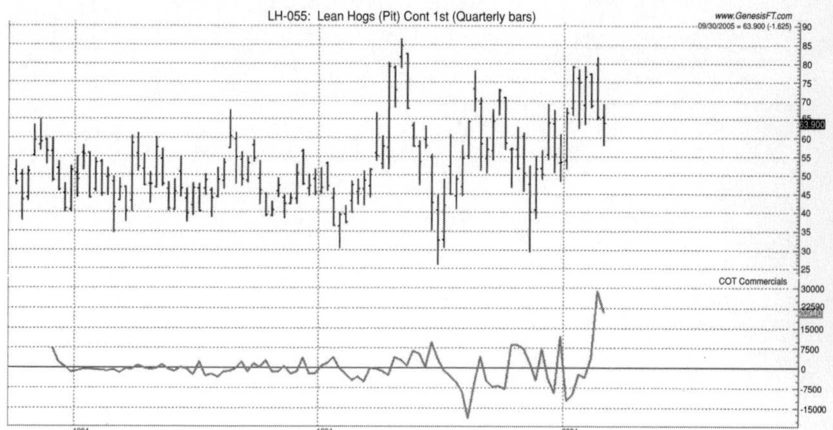

Source: Courtesy of www.GenesisFT.com.

4. Examine the chart and perform the tasks, and in questions A and B select the correct answer to the question in item C:

A. Indicate the points at which commercials had their largest net long positions.

B. Indicate the points at which commercials had their largest net short or hedged positions.

C. What happened after each instance of large net long positions by commercials?

i. Prices moved sideways.
ii. Prices went down.
iii. Prices eventually moved higher.
iv. Small traders went long.

5. Looking at the same chart, would you expect:

A. Expect prices to go higher.

B. Expect small traders to not trade this market.

C. Expect trading systems to be ineffective.

D. Expect this market to go much lower.

LESSON 17, DAYS 18–19

Commitment of Traders Report Part II: Triggers

The Commitment of Traders Report (COT) provides valuable information about pending changes in long-term trends. The report is only useful if you know how to understand the data it provides and how to apply it using triggers. This lesson shows you three triggers that can work very effectively with the COT commercials data. Remember that the method described here is not a fully automatic trading system but rather a methodology.

Not only does this method require some degree of judgment, but it requires patience since it attempts to capture large moves. My experience with the COT data is that it works best on all markets other than the financials (i.e., currencies, interest rate futures and stock index markets).

MAC TRIGGER

As you will recall from your previous lessons, the moving average channel (MAC) is a very effective way to catch the start of a new trend. Since the COT data are issued weekly, the best time frame to use for timing triggers with the COT is weekly. Accordingly, I suggest using a weekly MAC as one of the trigger methods for the COT. How does this work?

Here is a summary of the methodology:

- When the COT commercials net positions rises above the zero level, begin monitoring the weekly MAC for the given market.
- When the MAC gives a buy signal on the weekly chart, you can be a buyer.

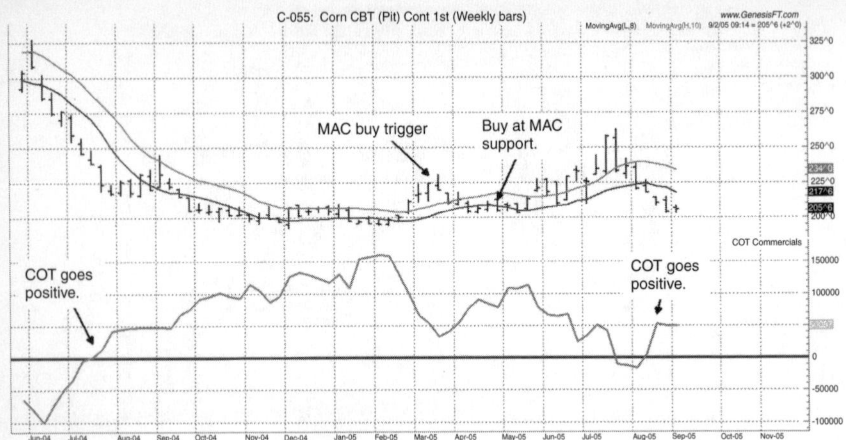

FIGURE 17.1 COT with MCA timing as a trigger.
Source: Courtesy of www.GenesisFT.com.

- Remember that this is an intermediate to long-term procedure. Since this is the case you can also attempt to buy if and when prices decline to MAC support.
- Use a trailing stop-loss procedure once you have achieved a profit.
- Exit the position if COT commercials go negative before you have achieved a profit.

Figures 17.1 and 17.2 offer annotated examples.

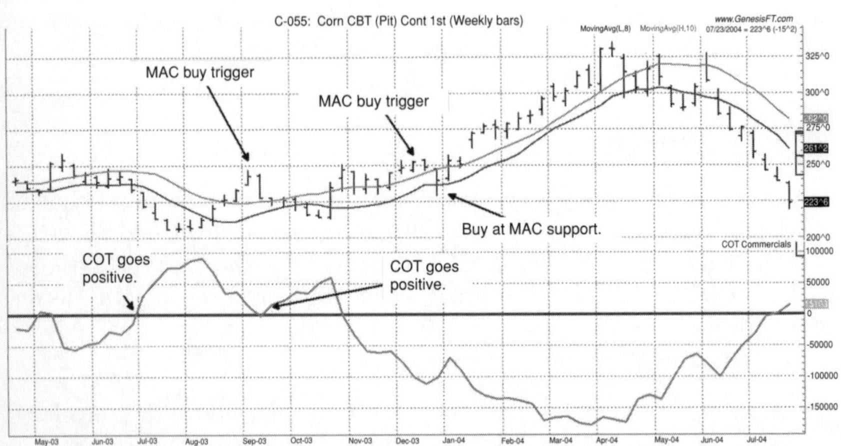

FIGURE 17.2 Another example of COT with MAC timing as a trigger.
Source: Courtesy of www.GenesisFT.com.

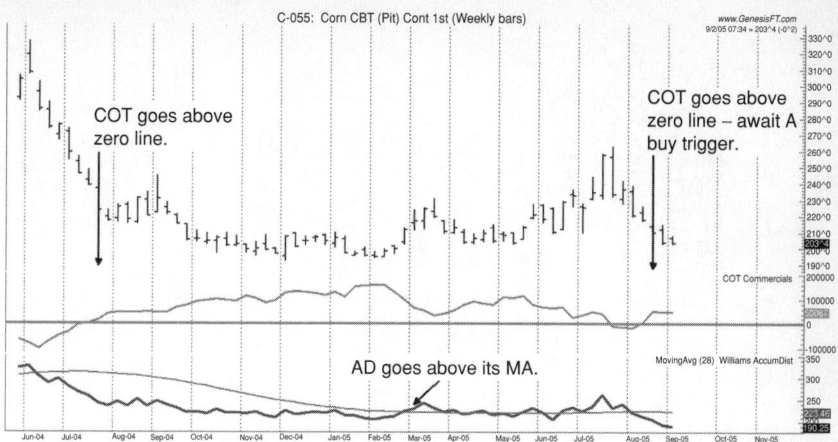

FIGURE 17.3 The ADMA with the COT commercials data.
Source: Courtesy of www.GenesisFT.com.

ACCUMULATION/DISTRIBUTION TRIGGER

When you study charts with COT and the MAC, you will see that this combination does not catch all of the moves. Accordingly, you may want to use the *accumulation/distribution moving average (ADMA)* as your timing trigger. The ADMA is a simple indicator that consists of the Williams accumulation/distribution (Williams AD) with a 28-period moving average (MA) of the indicator. Note that there are several indicators called accumulation/distribution. The one I use is the Williams AD. The timing trigger is simple. When AD goes above its MA a buy is triggered, and vice versa for a sell trigger. Figure 17.3 shows an example of the ADMA with the COT commercials data. As you can readily observe from my notations, ADMA can be used with the COT as a timing trigger.

Figure 17.4 gives yet another example of using the COT and the ADMA for timing.

Still another method that I have developed for using the COT commercials data as a timing method involves the following steps:

1. Plot a 19-period simple moving average of the commercials COT.
2. Plot a 9-period simple moving average of the 19-period moving average.
3. Use a weekly continuation chart of the markets you are studying.
4. Display only the two moving averages.

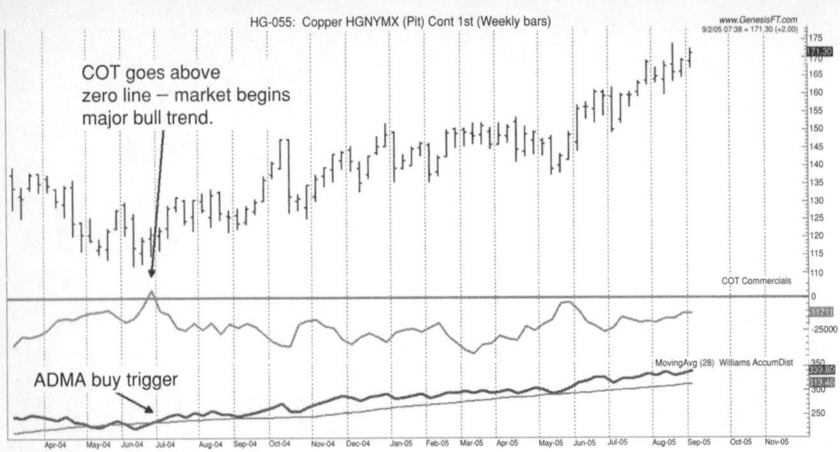

FIGURE 17.4 Using the COT ADMA for timing.
Source: Courtesy of www.GenesisFT.com.

5. When the shorter MA drops below the longer MA a buy is triggered.
6. When the shorter MA goes above the longer MA a sell is triggered.
7. Note that this is not the typical MA buy and sell relationship you are accustomed to. These triggers work the *opposite* way since commercials tend to be on the opposite side of the markets due to the nature of their business. The following two charts illustrate this method.
8. Note that since this is not a purely mechanical trading approach, you can change the moving average values to research other combinations that may be more effective.
9. Finally, remember that this is at the minimum an intermediate term method and at the maximum a long-term method. It therefore requires larger stop-losses and risks.

Figures 17.5 and 17.6 give two chart examples with annotations. Figure 17.7 shows this relationship with ADMA timing.

I believe that the effective use of COT data has not been given sufficient attention in the futures markets. There are other ways in which the COT can be used, and I encourage you to explore these ways.

REVIEW

This lesson completes our work on the COT indicator. I showed you three methods for timing markets for large moves using the COT commercials

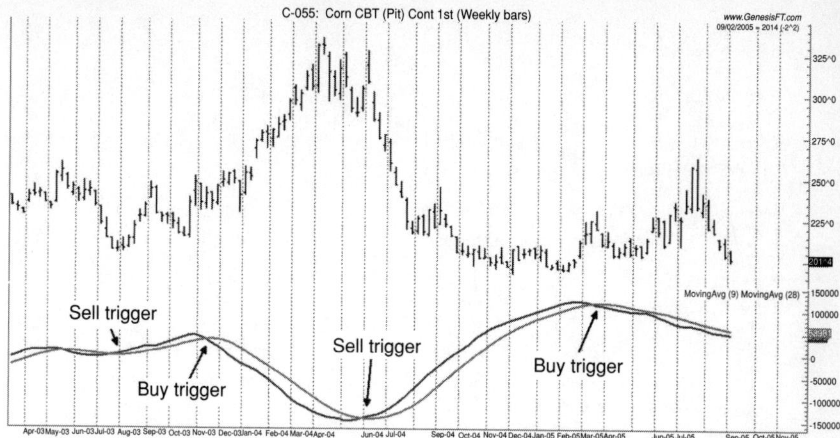

FIGURE 17.5 Using dual moving averages of the COT as a timing trigger.
Source: Courtesy of www.GenesisFT.com.

data. Please take a few minutes to answer the questions below. Note that this lesson's quiz requires more attention than some of the previous quizzes due to the fact that a degree of judgment is required when answering the questions that involve chart interpretation. Please take your time.

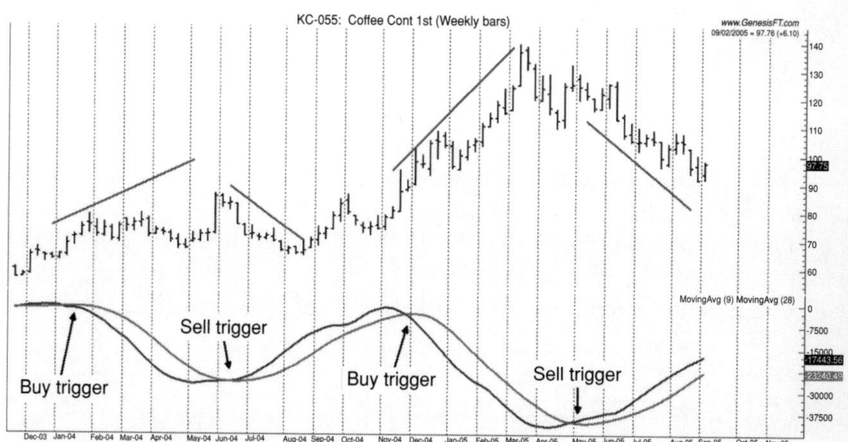

FIGURE 17.6 Another example of dual moving average COT as a timing trigger.
Source: Courtesy of www.GenesisFT.com.

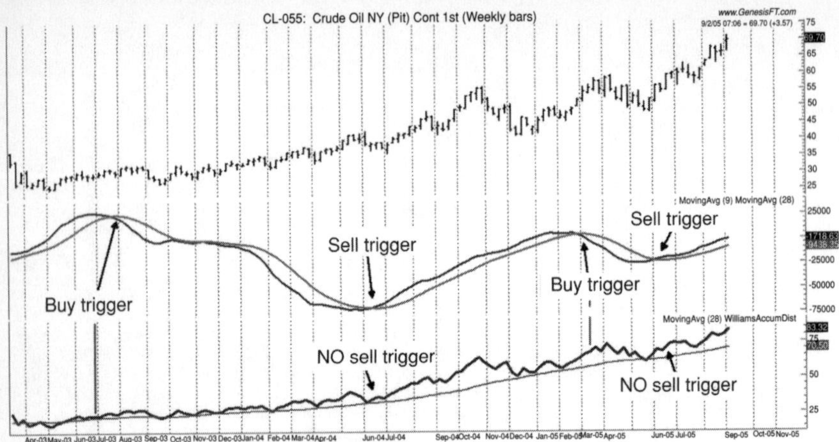

FIGURE 17.7 Combining the dual moving average of COT with the ADMA as a timing trigger.
Source: Courtesy of www.GenesisFT.com.

LESSON 17 QUIZ

Instructions: Follow the instructions carefully.

For items 1 through 3, mark the COT buy and sell signals as taught in this lesson.

1.

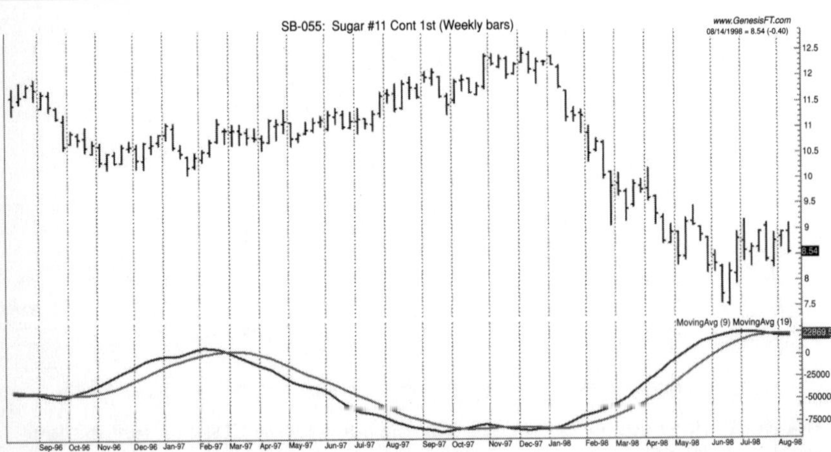

Source: Courtesy of www.GenesisFT.com.

2.

Source: Courtesy of www.GenesisFT.com.

3.

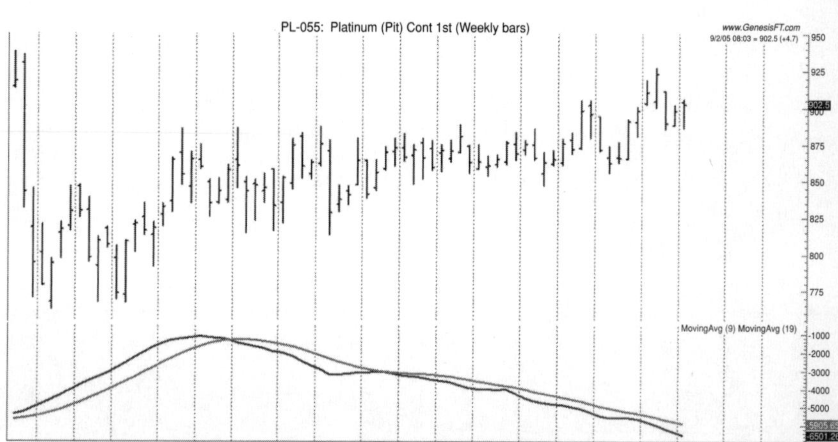

Source: Courtesy of www.GenesisFT.com.

For items 4 through 6, mark the triggers as described in this lesson.

4.

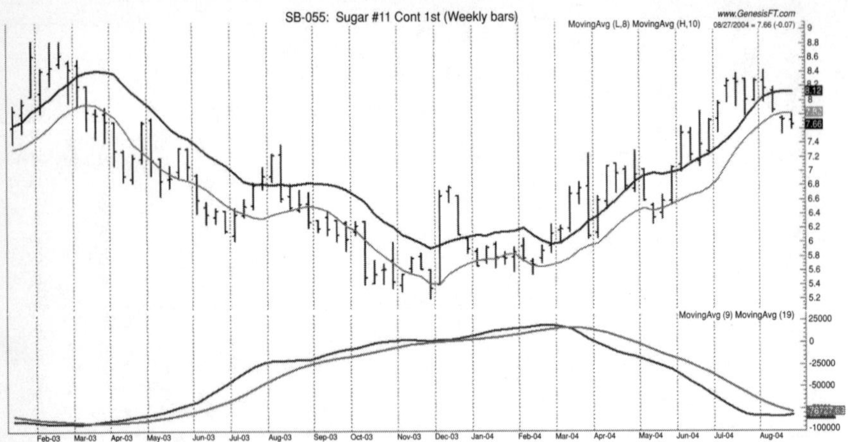

Source: Courtesy of www.GenesisFT.com.

5.

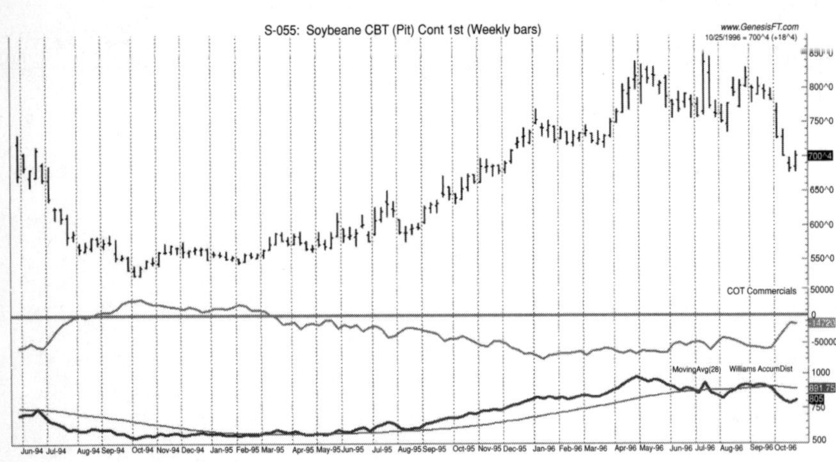

Source: Courtesy of www.GenesisFT.com.

6.

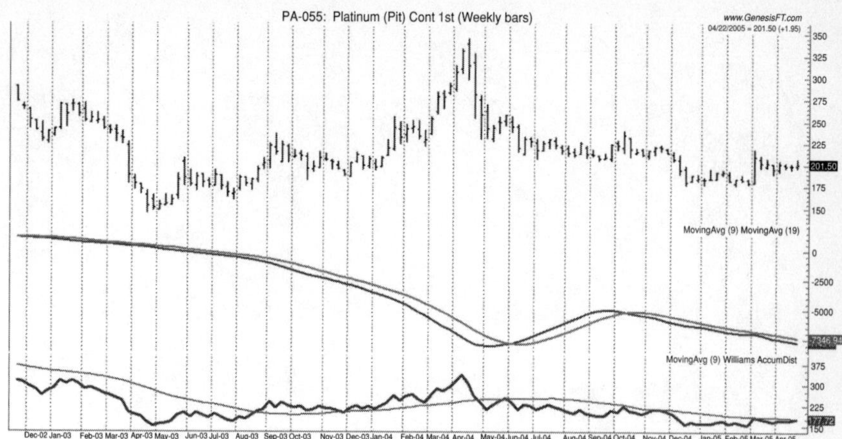

Source: Courtesy of www.GenesisFT.com.

LESSON 18, DAYS 20–21

The Advanced 30-Minute Breakout for S&P and E-mini Trading

The popularity of day trading in stocks and futures has been a blessing for many traders, but a curse to most. I say this because day trading is a difficult road to take as a means of making profits in stocks and futures. Previously in this course, I taught you the gap trade as a possible day-trading method.

This method requires very little attention. Most day-trading methods, however, require considerable attention. Although I advise you that day trading is both time consuming as well as difficult, there are ways in which to harness the profit potential of day trading. The 30-minute breakout method taught in this lesson will help you get the edge on day trading, but it will require the following:

- Maximum discipline and attention to rules.
- Persistence.
- At least $50,000 in starting capital for trading the full-sized S&P contract (less for E-mini S&P and other markets).
- The ability to accept at least seven consecutive losing trades.
- The ability to sit at the computer all day.
- The discipline to ride profits until the end of the trading day.
- The eventual ability to trade multiple positions.

THE CONCEPT AND SETUP

The *30-minute breakout method* (30MBO) uses the price high and price low of the first 30 minutes of each trading session (day session only) as the

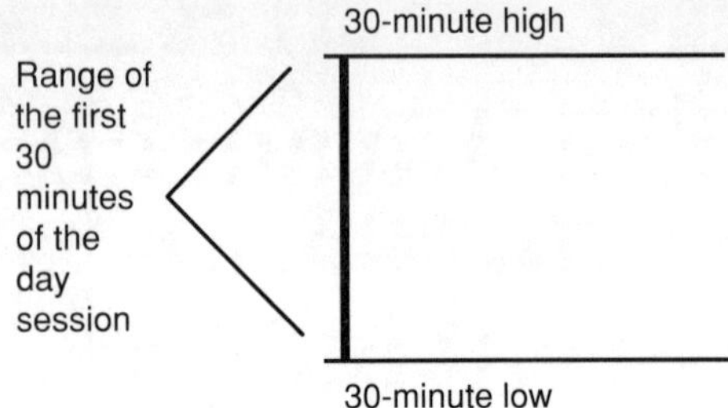

FIGURE 18.1 The 30MBO setup pattern showing the high and low of the first 30-minute price bar.

setup. The markets that are currently worth considering as appropriate for the 30MBO are S&P, E-mini S&P, and in stocks SPY, DIA, and QQQ.

Finding the setup is very simple. All you have to do is to make note of the high and low price for the first 30 minutes of the trading session; this can only be determined after the first half-hour is over. Figure 18.1 shows an example of this.

A buy trigger occurs when and if any subsequent 30-minute price bar *ends* above the high of the first 30-minute price bar. A sell trigger occurs when any subsequent 30-minute price bar *ends* below the low of the first 30-minute price bar. (Note my emphasis on *ends*.)

A trigger can only occur at the end of a bar, not during a bar. Figures 18.2 and 18.3 show two examples.

A trigger can occur at the end of any 30-minute bar up to, but no later than, the last hour of trading.

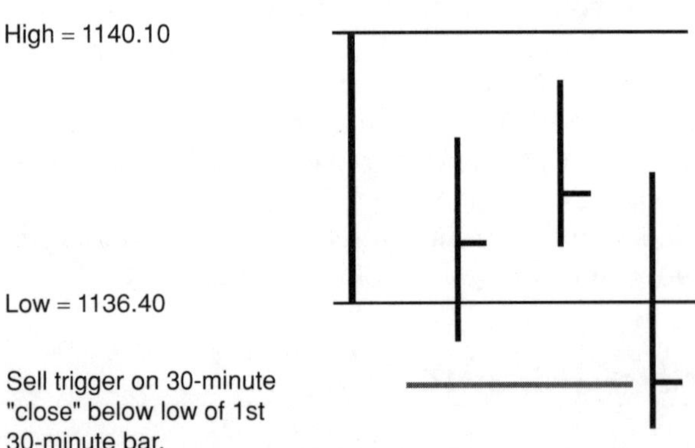

FIGURE 18.2 30MBO sell trigger example.

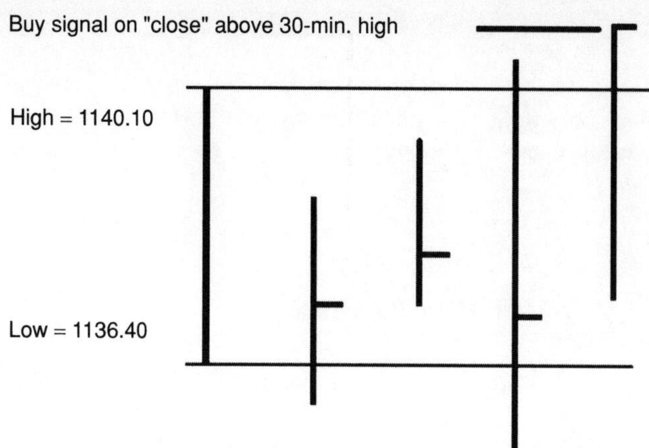

FIGURE 18.3 30MBO buy trigger example.

FOLLOW-THROUGH FOR THE 30MBO

Follow-through for the 30MBO is very simple, but you must be consistent and highly disciplined in order to employ the follow-through method profitably. Here are the rules:

- As soon as a trade has triggered, your stop-loss becomes the opposite side of the trade. In other words, if a buy is triggered first, then the stop is a 30-minute ending price below the low of the first 30-minute ending bar and vice versa for a short.
- When a trade is triggered, the first profit target is the *range* (high–low) of the first 30-minute bar.
- If you have multiple contracts, then take profit on part of your position at the first profit target and place a stop at breakeven.
- If and when the trade achieves twice the range of the first 30 minutes place a stop at the first profit target. If you have multiple positions, take profit on another portion of your position and place a stop at the first profit target.
- Exit MOC (market on close) on all positions not stopped out.
- If you get a buy first and are stopped out, then reverse to a sell and vice versa.
- Only take one reverse trade per day. In other words, if the second trade loses money then there are no additional trades for the day.
- Always exit at the end of the day.
- Data used are for the day session only.
- All entry orders are at the market.

This method can be very risky—but it can also produce some very large profits. The best time to begin using this method is after it has had 3–5 losses in a row.

EXAMPLES OF 30MBO TRADES

Figures 18.4 and 18.5 show examples of 30MBO trades from start to finish.

REVIEW

This lesson taught you the 30MOB method for day trading. The rules are clear and concise. Practice and the ability to ride large swings both in your favor and against you are of paramount importance if you want to be successful with this method.

Note that this lesson's quiz requires more attention than some of the previous quizzes due to the degree of judgment required when interpreting charts. Take your time.

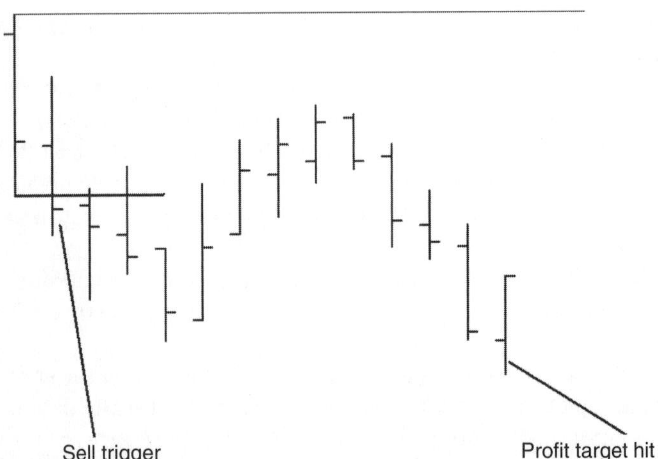

FIGURE 18.4 An example of the 30MBO setup, trigger, and follow-through.

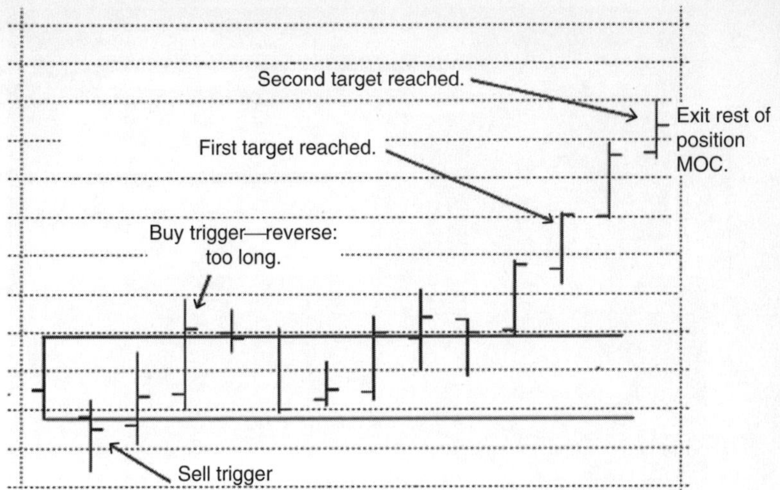

FIGURE 18.5 Another example of the 30MBO from trigger to exit.

LESSON 18 QUIZ

Instructions: Follow the instructions carefully.

Mark all the 30MBO signals as well as their follow-through. If you do not have the actual prices, use your best estimates.

1.

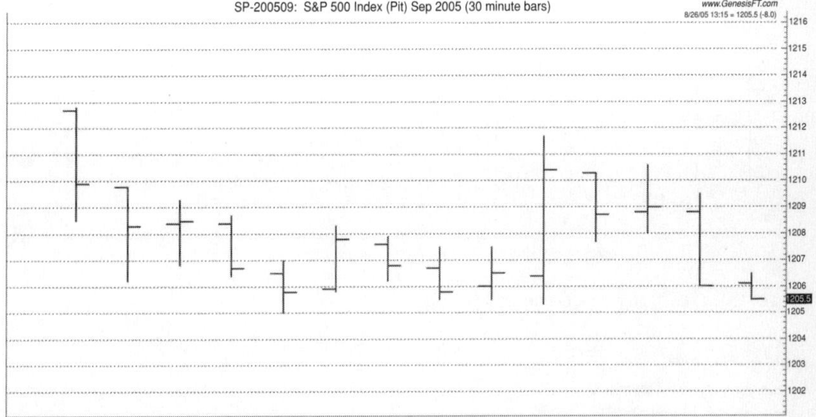

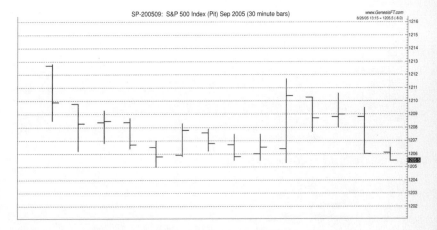

Source: Courtesy of www.GenesisFT.com.

2.

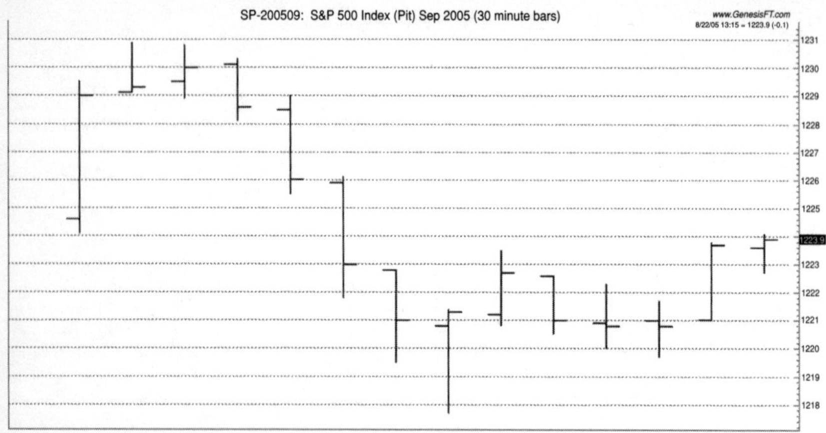

Source: Courtesy of www.GenesisFT.com.

3.

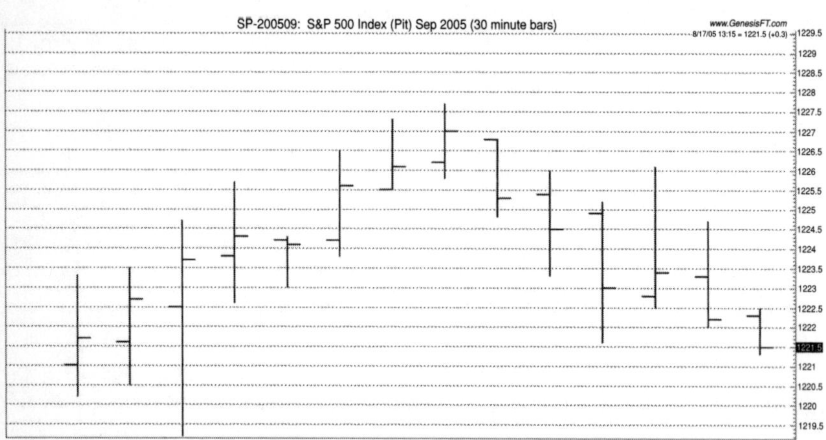

Source: Courtesy of www.GenesisFT.com.

4.

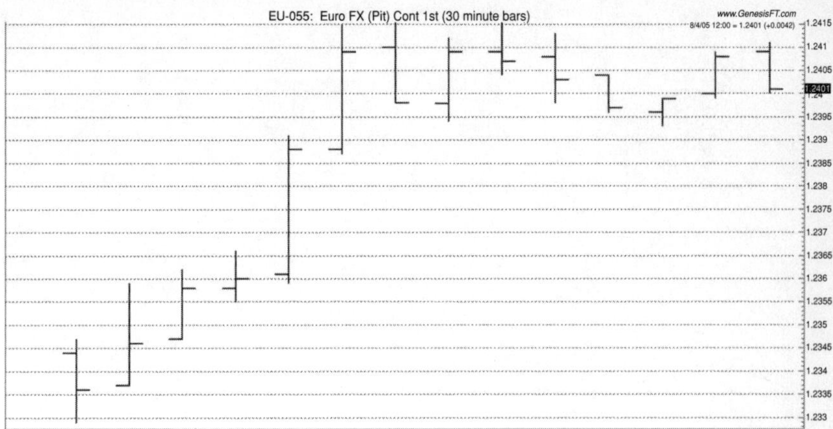

Source: Courtesy of www.GenesisFT.com.

5.

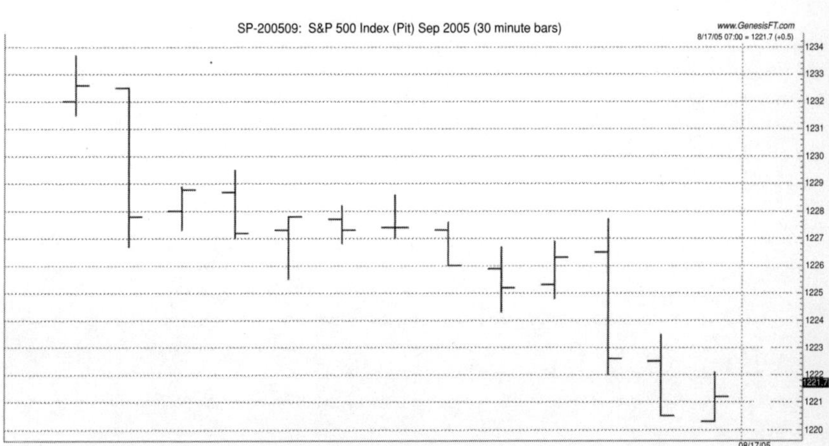

Source: Courtesy of www.GenesisFT.com.

6.

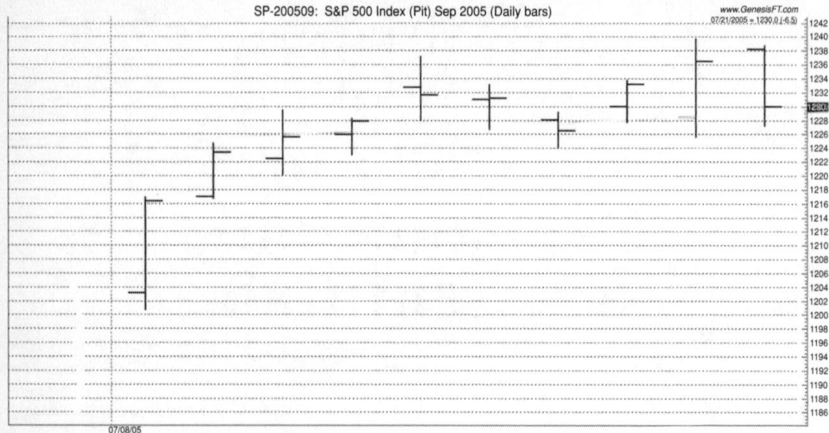

Source: Courtesy of www.GenesisFT.com.

LESSON 19, DAYS 22–24

How to Structure Your Trading Portfolio for Maximum and Consistent Gains

Here is the bottom line:

No matter how good your trading and timing methods are, you will not make money unless you can incorporate certain vital features into your trading.

In my 35 years of trading, investing, and market analysis I have observed that a vast majority of traders have no plan, no direction, and no structure in their trading. They trade by the seat of their pants hoping to make a profit. In point of fact, they limit their odds of doing so due to their lack of effective tools and procedures.

This lesson gives you the tools to help organize and implement your trades effectively and consistently. My suggestions here are not necessarily in their order of importance.

KEEP A TRADE LOG

Proper organization is a prerequisite to success. Many traders lose money because they are not organized. They are either unaware of trading signals when they occur or they are not prepared. The first thing you must do—and without fail—is to keep a record of every order that you enter. If you use online order entry, then the record of your orders will be there automatically.

However, if you do not, then you must use either a computerized trade (or order) log or a written one. The trade log should contain all relevant information for each order you enter.

Figure 19.1 gives an example of what your trade log should look like. You can easily set one up in any of the popular spreadsheet programs.

Here is how to use the trade log:

1. Assign each trade a number. The first trade of the day would be #1; the second trade of the day would be #2, and so on. Enter this number in the first column.
2. Indicate whether the trade is a Buy (B) or a Sell (S).
3. Indicate the type or order. For example, note if the order is at the market, MIT, limit, stop limit, day order, or market order. Use an abbreviation method such as M for market, D for day order, O for open order, L for limit, MI for MIT, and SL for stop limit.
4. Enter the market and contract month. In some cases you may also want to enter the exact time the order was placed and the ticket number your broker gives you. Do this if you are having difficulty getting good or timely fills from your broker.
5. Once the order has been filled, enter the price in the Fill or CXL column. If the trade is not filled and you cancel it, then enter CXL in this column.
6. You should be using a trading system or method. If so, then enter an abbreviation for the name of the system or signal in the Signal column so that you can keep track of your system or method performance and exit strategy.
7. Enter any relevant comments in the Comment columns. These notes should be as specific as possible so as to help you learn from your successes and failures.
8. Leave a *blank* line or lines after each trade so that you can fill it in when you exit the trade. The number of lines that you leave blank will be a function of the position size and system you are using. As you may recall, some of my methods exit positions one-third at a time. My illustration below will clarify if you are uncertain as to what I mean.
9. Once a trade has been closed out, enter the exit price and outcome in the indicated columns.
10. Use a new sheet for each day if you are keeping a paper trail.
11. It is best to use a computerized spreadsheet that will automatically give you a sum total of your profits and losses.
12. Compare your records with your brokerage statements to make sure that they are consistent.

Trading Record—Summary									
Market	Month	Method	Entry Signal B/S	Date In	Price	Date Out	Price	P/L	Notes

FIGURE 19.1 Trading record and order log.

13. Make certain that you keep track of open orders.
14. If you are trading several systems or methods, then I strongly recommend keeping a separate sheet for each as well as a separate account. It will make your recordkeeping easier and you will always know how the system is doing. If you mingle trades from different systems it will be difficult for you to parse out the performance of the different methods *and* you may have opposite trades in the same market which would cancel each other out.

Figure 19.2 gives an example of a completed trade log.

DIVERSIFICATION

If there is any one thing I can tell you that makes all the difference in the world it is this:

Diversification is one of the major keys to success in all trading and investing.

The fact of the matter is that unless you diversify your trades you will be very limited in the success you can achieve. What exactly is diversification? The "old school" thinking on diversification meant simply that you need to be in a variety of unrelated markets as opposed to "putting all of your eggs in one basket."

As an example, consider the following equity curve of a nondiversified trading method in Figure 19.3. Note the lack of stability in performance as well as the sometimes lengthy periods of decreasing net profits.

EQUITY CURVE WITHOUT DIVERSIFICATION

Figure 19.4 shows an equity curve of my *Grand Super System* (GSS), which is diversified on three levels (as discussed below). Note the significant difference between this curve and the undiversified approach shown above.

In reality things are not as simple as just one level of diversification. The "Jake school" of thinking on this subject is that there are at least three levels of diversification. These levels are described in the following sections.

Diversification across Markets

This level is the basic one and the application is simple:

Do not accumulate too heavy of a position in one market or in related markets.

If you want to diversify the seasonal method, for example, trade one of the meats, one of the grains, two unrelated currencies, one of the interest

Trading Record—Summary									
Market	Month	Method	Entry Signal B/S	Date In	Price	Date Out	Price	P/L	Notes
Gold (GC)	Dec-06	MAC	Buy	17-Nov	422.5	27-Dec	445.5	$2,300	Exited on trailing stop-loss.
Tnote (ZB)	Dec-06	Seasonal	Sell	19-Nov	108-10	30-Nov	108-00	$312.50	Out on exit date. Should have held with trailing stop
*Note: hypothetical trades.									

FIGURE 19.2 Example of a completed trade log.

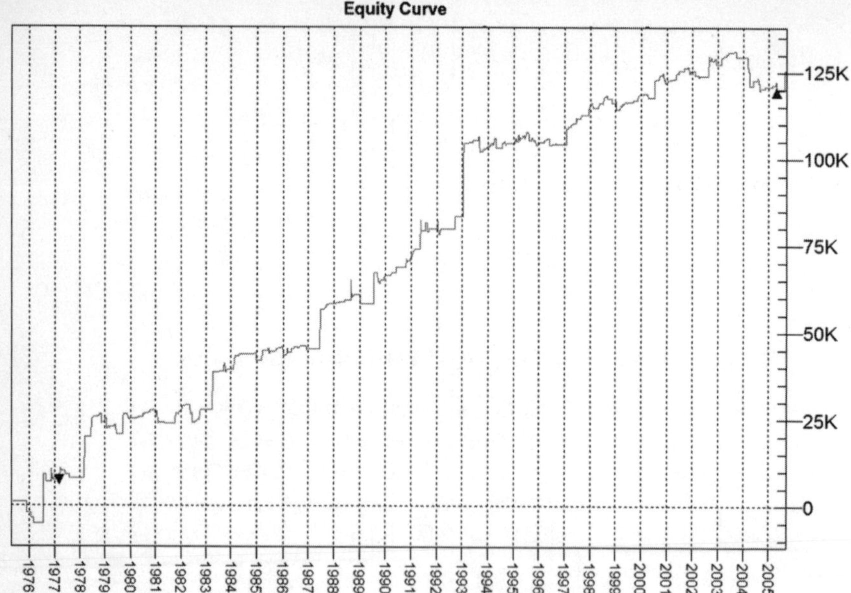

FIGURE 19.3 Equity curve.

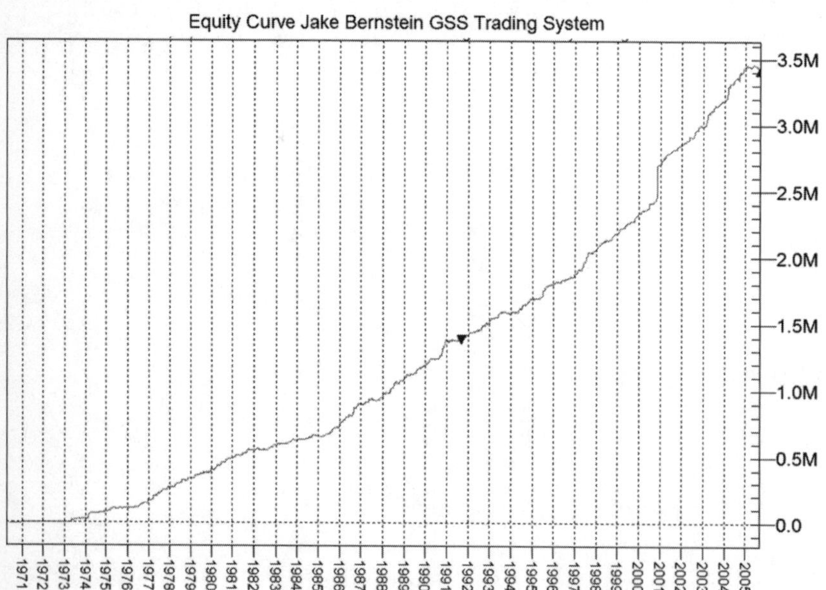

FIGURE 19.4 Equity curve without diversification.

rate futures markets, one of the precious metals, one of the energies, one of the interest rate futures, and the like. This approach will not weight you too heavily to closely correlated markets. In short, you will have balance, which will minimize losing streaks and sleepless nights.

Diversification across Time Frames

This is a level that very few traders talk about. The fact is that some markets are better for short-term trading while others are better for long-term or intermediate-term trading. Use the best market for the best time frame.

Diversification across Trading Methodologies

Some markets are more suitable for trading gaps, while other markets are better performers with momentum divergence. Wheat, for example, is primarily a seasonal market. It should therefore be traded primarily with seasonals. Wheat is also a good long-term market that works well with the COT approach discussed in previous lessons. Thus, you want to trade each market based on its best methodology.

I believe that diversification on all three levels will serve you best. You do not need a huge amount of money to do this. You can trade as few as three markets using this approach. The next lesson will give you considerably more details about diversification across time frames, markets, and methods.

REVIEW

This lesson taught you the importance of organization and recordkeeping. While these are not nearly as exciting as trading is, the lack of an effective and organized recordkeeping system can cost you dearly both in errors as well as in kissed opportunities.

Please take some time to answer this lesson's quiz questions.

LESSON 19 QUIZ

Choose the correct answer.

1. Proper organization of your trades is:
   - **A.** A prerequisite to success.
   - **B.** Necessary in order to avoid missing trades.
   - **C.** Helpful in keeping track of your performance.
   - **D.** All of the above.

2. Diversification is:
   - **A.** A trading system that uses diverse indicators.
   - **B.** Necessary if you want to spread risk and smooth out performance.
   - **C.** Only used by hedgers.
   - **D.** Automatically accomplished by using gap trades.
3. When using your Daily Trade log keep a record of:
   - **A.** Only trades that get filled.
   - **B.** Market on close orders.
   - **C.** Stop-losses and trailing stop-losses.
   - **D.** All trades and all orders.
4. The three levels of diversification are:
   - **A.** Setup, trigger, and follow-through.
   - **B.** Short-term trading, intermediate-term trading, and seasonals.
   - **C.** Diversification across markets, time frames, and trading methods.
   - **D.** MIT order, stop losses, and MOC orders.
5. It is best to segregate trades from different methods and systems into separate accounts because:
   - **A.** It will help you keep organized.
   - **B.** It will help you keep track of individual system performance.
   - **C.** It will avoid accidental liquidation of positions based on other methods.
   - **D.** All of the above.
6. Which of the following trading portfolios are diversified?
   - **A.** Cattle, gold, and T-notes.
   - **B.** Cattle, hogs, and feeder cattle.
   - **C.** S&P, soybeans, and cocoa.
   - **D.** Swiss franc, eurocurrency and U.S. dollar index.

LESSON 20, DAYS 25–27

Diversification

If there is anything in these lessons that I consider to be of the greatest importance, it is *diversification*. As I stated in the last lesson, your efforts will not be handsomely rewarded unless you are able to diversify your trading across time frames, across systems, and across markets. Whether you like it or not, this is a fact of market life. You may have been led to believe that if you become a specialist in one market, or in one system, that you will be successful. This is partially true. However, if the characteristics of that market change or if the market loses its popularity for *t* technical or fundamental reasons, then you are "up the creek without a paddle." In the medical profession, a specialist can do very well without the fear of being replaced. In trading, however, things are radically different. Naturally, opinions vary, but I have seen enough and done enough over my 35 years to know whereof I speak.

In the last lesson, I referred to the three levels of diversification: diversification across markets, diversification across time frames, and diversification across trading methods. I believe my approach to be very valid; however, the average trader has neither the experience nor the time to determine how to implement such a process. This lesson gives you some very pragmatic solutions to this issue.

THE BEST MARKETS FOR THE BEST TIME FRAMES

Some aspects of diversification are obvious while others are not so simple. For example, it is very clear that the most volatile markets are also the best markets for day trading and short-term trading. Volatility creates frequent changes and large price swings. Short-term traders and day traders thrive on such opportunities. Currently, the S&P, petroleum complex markets, some currencies and various U.S. and European interest rate futures offer the best prospects in these time frames.

On the other hand, determining which markets are best for intermediate and long-term moves is not as simple a proposition. You need to take into consideration the so-called "trendiness" of a market as well as the stability of the market within its trend. You could conduct lengthy and time-consuming research, or you can take advantage of my research, which is provided in this lesson. Some of the results may surprise you. For example, it turns out that Standard & Poor's is an excellent market for short-term trading as well as an excellent market for long-term trading. However, it is not as good as some markets for intermediate-term trading.

In addition, the lean hog market emerges as a very good candidate for short-term trading, contrary to what one might expect intuitively. The full results are contained in the synopsis of markets, systems, methods, and indicators discussed and summarized in the next section.

TYPES OF TRADING SYSTEMS

Figure 20.1 is a summary spreadsheet of markets, systems, methods, and indicators (which will be referenced again in this lesson's quiz). It offers a summary of my views on which markets work best in which time frames and with which methods. In order to understand it, though, a few definitions are in order.

> The truth about trading is that the markets are not linear in terms of systems and methods. That is, some markets are best suited for certain systems while others are not. Wheat, for example, is a terrible market for any short- or intermediate-term trading system unless it is based on seasonals. The T-bond and T-note markets are excellent systems for volatility breakout methods. The energies are fabulous markets for seasonals as well as trend-following systems, breakout systems, momentum divergence, and several others. You would not know any of this unless you had considerable experience or unless you have done considerable research.

Trend-Following Systems

Trend-following systems are essentially moving average–based systems that attempt to enter markets *after* a new trend has started. Because these

Market, System, Methods, and Indicators									
Market	Daily Gap	Mom Div	Mac	COT ADM	Time Frame	System Trading	Seasonal & Timing	Spreads & Timing	**Comments**
GRAIN AND SOYBEAN COMPLEX									
Corn	☺	☺	☺	☺	ALL	S	☺	☺	Primarily aseasonal market and best for LT, IT
Oats	×	☺	☺	☺	WM	S	☺	X	Primarily aseasonal market and best for LT, IT
Soybeans	☺	☺	☺	☺	ALL	S, L, I, V, Sw	☺	☺	Good market for most methods
Soybean Meal	☺	☺	☺	☺	ALL	S, I, L	☺	☺	Only use as a proxy for soybeans
Soybean Oil	×	☺	☺	☺	ALL	S, I, L	☺	X	Not a primary market-good for seasonals
Wheat	☺	☺	☺	☺	WM	S, I, L, Sw	☺	☺	Primarily aseasonal market and best for LT, IT
METALS									
Copper	☺	☺	☺	☺	ALL	ALL	☺	☺	Good market for most methods - some what erratic
Gold	☺	☺	☺	☺	ALL	S, I, L	☺	X	Primarily aseasonal market and best for LT, IT
Platinum/Palladium	x	☺	☺	☺	WM	S, I, L	☺	X	Primarily aseasonal market and best for LT, IT
Silver	☺	☺	☺	☺	ALL	S, I, L	☺	X	Primarily aseasonal market and best for LT, IT
CURRENCIES									
Br Pound	☺	☺	☺	X	ALL	ALL	☺	X*	Excellent in all areas except for intra-market spreads
Canadian $	☺	☺	☺	X	ALL	ALL	☺	X*	Excellent in all areas except for intra-market spreads
Japanese Yen	☺	☺	☺	X	ALL	ALL	☺	X*	Excellent in all areas except for intra-market spreads
Swiss Franc & Euro	☺	☺	☺	X	ALL	ALL	☺	X*	Excellent in all areas except for intra-market spreads
FIBERS/WOOD									
Cotton	☺	☺	☺	☺	ALL	ALL	☺	☺	Excellent in all areas
Lumber	☺	☺	☺	☺	ALL	S, I, L	☺	X	Excellent seasonals BUT low volume. CAREFUL !
SOFTS									
Cocoa	☺	☺	☺	☺	ALL	S, L, I, V, Sw	☺	X	Excellent in most areas except for spreads
Coffee	☺	☺	☺	☺	ALL	S, L, I, V, Sw	☺	☺	Excellent in all areas-BAD FILLS-be careful !
Orange Juice	X	☺	☺	☺	WM	S, I, L	☺	X	Seasonals are OK other wise IT and LT
Sugar	☺	☺	☺	☺	ALL	S, L, I, Sw	☺	☺	Excellent in most areas-usually lower risk
MEAT / LIVESTOCK									
Lean Hogs/LvCattle	☺	☺	☺	☺	ALL	ALL	☺	☺	Excellent in all areas especially spreads and seasonals
INTEREST RATE FUTURES									
EuroDollar	X	☺	☺	X	WM	x	☺	X	Excellent seasonals but very slow and steady
T-Bonds	☺	☺	☺	X	ALL	ALL	☺	☺*	Excellent in all areas and inter-market spreads
T-Notes	☺	☺	☺	X	ALL	ALL	☺	☺*	Excellent in all areas and inter-market spreads
STOCK INDEX FUTURES									
S&P 500/Dow	☺	☺	☺	X	ALL	ALL	☺	X	Excellent in most areas except for spreads
PETROLEUM COMPLEX									
All Energies	☺	☺	☺	☺	ALL	ALL	☺	☺	Excellent in most areas

Guide: M = Monthly W = Weekly T = Trend Following, SW = Swing
A = Accumulation Distribution ☺ = Good X = NO * = See Comment COT/ADM = COT + Accumulation/Dist MA
L = Long Term I = Intermediate Term S = Short Term © 2005 Jake Bernstein 800-678-5253

FIGURE 20.1 Summary spreadsheet of markets, systems, methods, and indicators.

systems tend to enter after the start of a trend, they are generally low in accuracy and all too often have numerous consecutive losing trades.

They are not the best systems you can use, but they do make money if you can cope with low accuracy and large drawdowns.

Volatility Breakout Systems

Volatility breakout systems are based on the idea that markets tend to move in sideways patterns that, from time to time, break out in one direction or another. These are generally good systems with higher accuracy.

Breakout Systems

Breakout systems are systems that tend to buy when prices have penetrated given resistance levels and sell when prices have penetrated given support levels. Depending on how they determine support and resistance levels, they can be very accurate systems.

Seasonal Systems

Seasonal systems use seasonality and timing. These are among the most accurate systems if used correctly.

Swing Trading Systems

Swing trading systems are generally short-term systems that attempt to buy at support in uptrends and sell at resistance in downtrends. These are usually very good systems if they are based on valid and reliable trend indicators.

Divergence Systems

Divergence systems are based on divergence between prices and indicators. These are excellent systems for most markets if they are based on appropriate divergence indicators that combine effective follow-through methods.

Price Pattern Systems

Price patterns such as gaps, 30-minute breakout, the 8OC, reversals, and the like are often excellent short-term methods if their logic is solid. Unfortunately there are many traditional price patterns for which validity has not been verified and which should not be used.

Market Geometry Systems, Astrology-based Systems, and Market Structure Theories

Market geometry systems such as Gann, Elliott, Fibonacci, and the like are not reliable because they are often subject to numerous different interpretations. My advice is to steer clear.

Astrology-based systems should be avoided entirely. I see absolutely no validity on these methods.

Market structure theories such as the Market Profile™ or Liquidity Bata Bank™ have great potential, but they require serious study and analysis before they can be turned into objective trading systems. They are highly complex and beyond the scope of this book. There are other systems as well. These, however, are among the most popular.

REVIEW

This lesson discussed diversification and its implementation on three different levels. Now that you have been exposed to my views on diversification, I advise you to review the methods and systems taught in the preceding lessons and to construct your own diversified portfolio. Remember that you can do this with as little as three markets and limited capital.

The lesson quiz that follows tests you on using the Market Systems, Methods and Indicators Spreadsheet in Figure 20.1 in at least eight markets that are good for seasonal trading while timing your ability to create a diversified portfolio. Let us see how you do!

LESSON 20 QUIZ

Instructions: Circle the correct answers.

1. Which of the following are correct?
   - **A.** Some markets work better in certain timeframes than in others.
   - **B.** S&P is a good market for day trading and for COT.
   - **C.** Currencies are not good markets for short-term trading.
   - **D.** Wheat is a primarily seasonal market.
2. Astrology-based systems:
   - **A.** Are highly effective.
   - **B.** Are not reliable based on my experience.
   - **C.** Only used by hedgers.
   - **D.** Are best used with COT.

3. Volatile markets:
   - A. Are good for seasonal trading.
   - B. Are good for the Market Profile™ method.
   - C. Are good for day trading and short-term trading.
   - D. Are best for new traders.
4. Using the Market Systems, Methods, and Indicators Spreadsheet in Figure 20.1, construct a diversified portfolio of four markets and list them below:

   ____

   ____

   ____

   ____

5. Using the Market Systems, Methods, and Indicators Spreadsheet in Figure 20.1, list at least eight markets that are good for seasonal trading with timing:

   ____

   ____

   ____

   ____

   ____

   ____

   ____

   ____

6. Why is the oats market not suitable for day trading?
   - A. It is a new market and does not have enough historical data.
   - B. It is primarily used by cattle producers to hedge positions.
   - C. It is not sufficiently volatile.
   - D. It only moves with the currency markets.
7. Using the Market Systems, Methods, and Indicators Spreadsheet in Figure 20.1, list a diversified portfolio using at eight markets:

   ____

   ____

   ____

   ____

   ____

   ____

   ____

   ____

LESSON 21, DAY 28

Putting It All Together

If you have survived the last 20 lessons and learned from them, then I truly believe that you have in your possession some of the most powerful tools that a trader can possess. These tools, combined with the discipline and consistency that the setup, trigger, and follow-through structure provide should bring you excellent results. I have spent very little time teaching and preaching to you about the psychological and behavioral pitfalls that can limit your profits or, at worst, cause you to take losses no matter how good your systems, methods, or indicators may be.

This next-to-last lesson—which is not be followed by a quiz—will put things together for you by giving you a list of dos and don'ts, not necessarily in order of importance. If you adhere to the methods that I taught you in these lessons, follow the STF structure, and observe and implement the rules and procedures in this lesson, you will increase your odds of success dramatically.

WHY TRADERS LOSE

In my over 35 years of trading, teaching, and analyzing markets, I have had literally hundreds of opportunities to observe my mistakes and the mistakes of other traders. Human nature is a curious thing. It is at one and the same time wonderful and sad. It is wonderful because we can do so much with our minds. It is sad because all too often our minds keep us from being successful. Here are some of the reasons that traders lose money in spite of their otherwise good trading systems:

- Insufficient starting capital. Too many traders begin with a very small amount of capital and attempt to trade too many markets. Beginning with a small amount of money and attempting to trade too many markets is an invitation to failure.
- Lack of a system or method. This has been discussed extensively in preceding lessons.
- Lack of organization, which causes traders to make impulsive decisions.
- Trading on the advice of a broker.
- Spreading a position to avoid taking a loss.
- Buying out-of-the-money options.
- Trading too often.
- Taking quick profits and riding losses.
- Failure to maximize profits on each trade.
- Using too many indicators.
- Getting trading suggestions in Internet chat rooms.
- Getting too many recommendations from too many newsletters.
- Adding to losing positions to average your cost.
- Pyramiding positions by adding larger numbers of contracts as prices move in your favor.
- Failure to know what kinds of orders to use and when to use them.
- Using stop-losses that are too small for the volatility in the market you are trading.
- Day trading for small profits.
- Lack of a trading plan.
- Failure to follow the STF model.
- Impatience.
- Inability to follow a trading method when it suffers a few consecutive losses.
- The mistaken belief that all trading indicators are worthwhile.
- Overoptimizing trading systems.
- Attempting to trade in too many time frames and in too many markets at once.
- Playing with "scared money" (money you cannot afford to lose).
- Watching every price tick all day long.

There are probably even more losing behaviors those traders can engage in, but I think I have covered the vast majority of them.

WINNING BEHAVIORS

As you can see from the partial list above, there are many things traders can do that will virtually guarantee them losses. The list of positive or winning behaviors is a very short one. It is, nevertheless, a very important one.

Here are the behaviors and procedures you will want to incorporate and internalize in your trading. They will not guarantee success but they will facilitate it!

- Use the STF structure for all trades you make . . . or
- Use a totally mechanical trading system that uses solid rules not open to interpretation.
- Be totally organized, by which I mean know all your trades, all your positions, all your orders at all times.
- Learn what different order types mean and how they are used.
- Avoid broker opinions and Internet chat rooms.
- Play your own game unless you have a trading partner or partners.
- Avoid reading more than one or two newsletters or hotlines.
- Avoid day trading unless you can do it full time.
- Diversify your trades across time frames, systems, and markets.
- Plan your trades and trade your plans.
- Begin with sufficient capital.
- Don't overextend your margin.
- Be willing to accept as many as seven consecutive losing trades.
- Don't trade more—trade less.
- Segregate your trades from different methods into separate accounts.
- Avoid the popular radio and television business shows—the odds are that if you're following valid systems and the STF structure, you know more than the so-called experts can tell you.

WHAT'S NEXT?

This lesson is not followed by a quiz. Now that you have worked through the lessons, take some time to sit back and evaluate the methods within your financial ability, time frame, discipline, and individual psychology. You must enjoy the methods you are using and you must understand them. Unless you do so, you will not want to follow the methods.

Take your time, plan your trades, and trade your plans.

Lesson 22 will discuss the Psychology and Discipline of Trading. It is perhaps the most important lesson in this course. Study it well, and you will avoid the many pitfalls that can affect the traders' bottom-line performance.

LESSON 22, DAYS 29-30

The Psychology and Discipline of Trading

If you have been trading stocks or commodities for even a relatively short period of time, then you are well aware of the fact that psychology and discipline are the weakest links in the trading chain. No education and trading would be complete without a discussion of the most important aspects of psychology and discipline.

This lesson gives you tools that you need to put the methods and systems that I have discussed into action. Here are some very important thoughts and considerations that will help you minimize the negative effects of trader psychology while maximizing the positives. Think them through carefully and give them the serious attention they deserve. Then, if you feel that they make sense to you or if you "see" yourself in some of the behaviors I have discussed, then make the necessary corrections.

This final lesson is not followed by a quiz. The true and final test of your ability and willingness to incorporate these suggestions into your trading plan will be your results.

ENEMIES OF THE TRADER

As traders and investors, we are always struggling with the demons that denigrate performance or that cause us to lose money. The best trading tools are useless in the hands of an undisciplined trader whereas a mediocre or "ugly duckling" trading approach can be transformed into a money-making swan. The critical variables that differentiate winners from losers are not on a function of the pragmatic considerations I cited earlier but they are also related to the internal and/or behavior factors that affect the trader. The "enemies" of the trader are usually those that reside deep within the psyche of the trader or in learned behavior patterns that may have served their purpose at one time but which are no longer functional at this time.

Trading and investing are, at best, difficult undertakings and, at worst, losing propositions. Yet in spite of the difficulties, the allure, the intrigue, and the possibility of striking it rich continue to attract traders the world over. Unfortunately, many of the newcomers lack the trading skills as well as the trading discipline. Jesse Livermore (alias Edwin LeFèvre) expressed it eloquently as follows: "The chief enemies of the trader are always boring from within."

What or who are these "chief enemies"? How can we recognize them? How can we "locate" and eradicate them? Are there proven methods for doing so? There are many roadblocks to successful trading. In fact, several books could be written about the factors that limit success but fewer yet on the factors that facilitate success. There are literally hundreds of things traders can do that will lose them money. There are only a few things that lead to profits.

I have summarized the major "loss producing" factors (i.e., the enemies of the trader) for you as shown below. While I am certain that there are many who disagree with my conclusions, I have drawn on my many years of personal experience in my own trading as well as my observations of thousands of traders the world over. Here is a synopsis of my findings. It is followed by a brief commentary about each.

Imagination

An active imagination can prove highly beneficial to a fiction writer, an artist, or a musician, but it has no place in trading. Many traders are prone to overly active imaginations. They envision or create positive as well as negative scenarios. Both can be destructive because they may lead to unrealistic conclusions and expectations. It is best for the trader to avoid imagining possible outcomes for a given trade.

To counteract this tendency, the trader must rely on his or her trading methodology to the exclusion of all other expectations. Once you have entered a trade, do not allow your imagination to rule your emotions or your expectations.

Overthinking

Overthinking is a form of an overly active imagination, albeit in a more concrete or intellectual way. Once you have developed a trading system or method, and once you have entered a trade, all the thinking or analysis in the world will not change the outcome of that trade. In fact, too much thinking may cause you to lose your confidence, thereby prompting you to make a costly error that is not based on your original methodology.

Avoid creating "if-then" scenarios. Avoid talking or thinking in phrases such as "If I had only," or "I should have" or "What if" or "If I added more indicators to my system then ..." Other statements to avoid are "Looks like the market wants to ..." or "I think it is time to get in." This type of analysis should be done when developing a system, *not* after a trade has been entered and *not* after your system has indicated that a trade should be entered. The market does not care what you think. The market will "do its own thing" no matter what you think and no matter how strongly you think that it "looks like it wants to go up."

Overdosing on the News

The amount of news that is available on the markets is staggering, and it is growing larger by the second. The rapid growth of Internet communications, blogs, websites, and e-mail has created a "news overload" situation. There is so much news out there that it can often be confusing and even misleading. Experts are plentiful. Newsletters abound. Opinions are available virtually everywhere.

Traders have a love-hate relationship with news. They love the news when it supports their position in the market(s) and they hate the news when it is contrary to their position in the market(s). Unless you know the news before it happens, or unless you are the person making the news, the odds are that it will not help you make money.

As market technicians, we expect that our indicators and methods will let us know when markets are likely to change direction or that they have changed direction. Most market technicians believe that their methods are sensitive enough to detect the behavior of insiders before the markets make their moves. We believe technical indicators will tell us the impact of the news and not the news itself. As a technical trader, I advise you to avoid being exposed to the news if you are prone to be swayed to deviate from your system or trading plan. The news can be your best friend and your worst enemy. Try to avoid either of these extremes.

Fight Your Fear

Fear is the most serious enemy of the trader. It can cause you to avoid making a trade and it can cause you to exit a trade too soon. The time to be fearful about a trade is *before* you enter it. Once it has been entered, your fate is sealed. Let the trade run to its logical conclusion as prescribed by your system or method. Do not get out too soon and do not get out too late. Simply stated, follow the rules and they will eliminate the fear, or, at the very least, minimize it.

The best antidote for fear is confidence. Confidence does not just happen. It is the product of an effective trading strategy. If you have confidence in your methods then you will have less fear. And less fear will bring more profits through less error.

Keeping Greed in Check

Greed is not as serious an enemy as fear, but it runs a close second. Greed can also prove to be your greatest enemy by causing you to stay with a trade after it should be closed out. When it is time to get out of a trade, then get out. Do not hold on, attempting to force the last drop of money out of the trade.

Furthermore, do not accumulate a larger position on any market if your finances and risk will not allow it. Having too large a position at the wrong time can and will destroy you.

Managing Expectation

If there is anything you should rightfully expect after you put on a trade it is that you will take a loss. Beyond this any profit you make is confirmation and affirmation that your methodology is effective and that you are able to execute it thoroughly. Expect the worst-case scenario, not the best! Expectation falls into the category of "imagination" as discussed above. Be less imaginative and more mechanical.

Avoiding Rationalization

One of the worst things a trader can do is to avoid taking responsibility for his or her losses. It is very tempting to blame everyone but yourself. Do not try to explain away your losses by resorting to all manner and sorts of excuses. You lost on a trade either because your system or method was wrong or because you didn't follow the rules. You must assume full responsibility in order to facilitate learning by correcting your error(s). There is always the temptation to blame your broker, or your trading advisor, or a newsletter writer or a friend. There are no excuses. Most traders have a repertoire of excuses that grows with each loss. Forget about making excuses—they are not productive.

The Price of Disorganization

Some of the biggest mistakes I have made in my trading have been caused by disorganization. I have missed trades, lost trades, misplaced orders, forgotten to put in stops and worse, all due to disorganization.

Make it your goal to be organized and disciplined in your market studies. If you use a system or method, then make certain you update it regularly. Keep good track of the trades you've made. Forgetting to enter or exit a trade due to disorganization can prove costly.

HOW TO THINK AND ACT LIKE A PRO

Now that we have examined some of the enemies of the trader, let us look at some of the positives behaviors you can develop.

Get Organized

Organization is vital to the success of any venture. It is important to know where you are headed, when you expect to get there, and which vehicles you will use to reach your destination. Without organization, these tools can often be misplaced. Your charts, books, formulae, trading rules and telephone numbers, and the like must be readily available.

Develop Discipline

This is, of course, easier said than done. There are many ways in which it can be achieved. One of them is to take a course on self-improvement, such as those offered by the Dale Carnegie Institute. You will learn that success requires discipline and that discipline can be learned. Discipline can often be improved through the simple application of behavioral learning techniques. My book, *The Investors Quotient* (New York: John Wiley & Sons, 1980) gives specific suggestions and techniques designed to help you improve your discipline. In addition, there are many simple exercises that you can use.

Remember that discipline from one area of your life tends to be reflected in all others. Therefore, if you lack self-discipline when it comes to changing such negative habits as overdrinking, overweight, overeating, and smoking, then you will probably lack the discipline required for successful trading. You may need to overcome these habits first, or you may need to conquer all lack of discipline at once.

Finally, remember that discipline is not synonymous with rigidity. Being rigid in following rules is not necessarily a form of discipline. Being a disciplined trader also means being flexible enough to change course as soon as you see that the action you have taken is not working. The rigid trader will believe too strongly in his or her trading rules and this can prove destructive. Trading is a game of probability, and there is no room for rigidity when it comes to probability.

Develop a Simple and Effective Trading Approach

One of the greatest limitations on success in trading is that systems become too complicated, too burdensome, or too time-consuming to use. If you build a boat, make certain you can get your boat into the water. Once in the water, make certain you can move.

Too many traders spend too much time developing complicated, sophisticated "trading systems" that are too difficult to implement. My knowledge of top-ranking, successful futures traders shows that most of them use simple methods. You will hear "keep it simple" repeated again and again.

"Keep it simple" is one of the foremost rules. If you keep it simple you are less consumed with details, less troubled with self-discipline, and you shorten your market response time. This alone will prove very valuable. Therefore, keep it simple!

Keep Impulsive Trading to a Minimum—Stay Relatively Isolated

There is a great deal to be said for isolationism in trading. In order to keep free of impulse, it is often best to not know the news. Then you can (as the saying goes) keep your head while all those around you are losing theirs. You will, in so doing, avoid the costly errors that are so often the result of impulsive behavior rather than following your system.

I favor isolation. I prefer not to listen to the radio or television news, not to read the newspapers, not to discuss the markets, not to listen to the opinions of others and not to discuss the markets, even with other professionals. I do this because I know that I may have weaknesses. In order to be strong and avoid impulsive actions motivated by the emotions of fear and/or greed, I must limit my exposure to extraneous information.

Plan Your Trades and Trade Your Plans

This market cliché is just as true today as when it was coined. It is the best way to avoid virtually all of the losing inputs. If you are prepared, and if you act according to your plan, you will have taken the first and most important step to practicing self-discipline.

Keep Your Objectives Clearly in Mind

You must always keep your goals in mind. If you are a short-term trader, then you must think and act like one. However, if you are a long-term trader, then your perception of the markets and your corresponding actions must be consistent with these objectives. I have found it best to have a list of objectives and goals handy for quick reference during in times of need.

Vent Frustration and Relieve Stress—Do Not "Live the Markets"

In order to improve market decisions, it is necessary to deal effectively with stress. There are many ways in which this can be achieved. Exercise is one good way to cope with stress. It can help you vent frustrations and give you a chance to get your mind off the markets. Furthermore, leave the markets at the office.

If you plan to trade as your profession, then this rule is vital. If you plan to trade in your spare time, then have certain hours set aside for this activity and do not become a market addict.

TO THINK OR NOT TO THINK: THE TRADER'S DILEMMA

In closing this lesson on trader psychology and discipline, I leave you with a little bit of controversy. In 1969, when I made my first futures trade, thinking and analysis were fashionable. The 1960s and 1970s were good times for thinkers, freethinkers, thought-provoking issues, civil disobedience, and analytical traders. Thinkers thought great thoughts about the future of our nation, about our presence and purpose (if any) in Vietnam, about domestic and international policy, racial issues, concerns about freedom and equality, and concern about the poor and the homeless. Thinking prompted radical action by various political interest groups. Frequent and violent antiwar protests disrupted the social structures of our nation. Civil disobedience, draft card burnings, sit-ins and student protests were the rule and not the exception. The fundamentals that moved stock and futures prices were studied closely. They were analyzed, scrutinized, and theorized. Computer analysis of the markets was a new and promising science. Thy "why" question was paramount in the minds of traders and investors.

Against the backdrop of this intellectual Zeitgeist, we were taught that if success was to be through trading we would need to consider each trade carefully; all potential outcomes were to be critically evaluated in terms of risk and reward; cause and effect. Trading decisions, we were told, which were the result of intensive analysis were likely to be more correct than those which were the product of less intensive scrutiny. In fact, thinking about trades was so much in vogue that traders would frequently seek out numerous sources of information in order to validate each of their trades. There was no such thing as "too much information." After all, how could there be too much information in the so-called Information Age?

While the idea that more information results in more profits seems logical on the surface, the actual result could be less profits. Why? Consider the following discussion.

EDSEL TRADING

Do you remember the story of the Edsel? In what seemed to be a reasonable, logical, and very intelligent approach, Ford Motor designed the Edsel to please the consumer. They did so by attempting to include all the features that the public wanted in a vehicle. The end result was a car that failed miserably. The simple truth is that "too many cooks spoil the broth." Consider the following questions with regard to trading:

- How much information is enough? Do you really need to subscribe to six newsletters? Have your numerous daily visits to Internet advisory Web sites proved productive? Have you gotten good information from business television and radio shows? Does the vast amount of available information help you or does it confuse you?
- How can you decide when you have given a trading decision sufficient thought or analysis? Does it take you more than a few minutes to make a decision? Do you vacillate when making your decisions? Do you change your mind once you have decided on a plan of action? Do you consult your broker as the final check and balance on your trades?
- Are there any objective measures for knowing when you have thought about something enough, or does the process end when things "feel right"? Do you use a mechanical trading system to determine your market entry and exits? Are you a "discretionary trader"? By this I mean do you use multiple technical inputs to help you reach a decision?
- Is there a correlation between the amount of thought devoted to a trade and its end result? Do you get less return for more effort?
- Do your intensive analysis and thought truly lead to success in trading, or do you expend ten units of energy and effort for one unit of return?

THINGS TO CONSIDER

There are literally thousands of things that a trader can do in the markets. Unfortunately, there are few winning choices and many losing ones. Obviously, our primary goal in creating success is to maximize the positives and minimize the negatives. There is no single answer to the resolution of this dilemma; rather there are several or even numerous answers. In addition, the answers vary from one trader to another as a function of their personality, individual limitations, market orientation, and available capital.

What follows are some points to consider in your plan to find effective methods and systems that will dovetail with your individual abilities. In so doing, consider the following issues and suggested solutions.

Deep Thought: Friend or Foe?

What is deep thought to one trader is either a mere pittance to another trader or a totally worthless activity to yet another trader. There are no set standards, no guarantees, and no insurance policies that your efforts will yield profits. There is no firm correlation between the amount of thought and deliberation that goes into a trade and the outcome of that trade. In fact, if there *is* a correlation, then it is likely an inverse one. Less is often more in the markets. Simplicity is better than complexity.

Decisions made seemingly off the cuff by some traders are often more successful than decisions made by committees. Computers have totally revolutionized the decision-making process by doing our "thinking" for us. Once the computer has done the hard work there's really nothing left to do but to take the prescribed action. If you are using a trading system of method that has proven its efficacy either by your actual experience with it or through historical back testing then any hesitation subsequent to the acquisition of the trades is hesitation that will surely lead to confusion, indecision, insecurity, ambivalence, and equivocation—none of which are constructive inputs in the formula for success.

Why Bother?

The purpose of my comments is to make a case for "simpler" and "less intelligent" trading. I have stated my view on this issue earlier, however, I would like to underscore its importance in this section. Once the facts about a trade are known and once the computer has decided on the best course of action, there is no choice for you but to take action, provided that the degree of risk is acceptable. Failure to take action constitutes a breach of the "contract" between you and the computer, but more importantly between you and yourself. I suggest that the failure to act on your system is the first indication that you have taken a wrong turn, which will eventually lead you down the road to ruin unless you change things.

Learning to Change

The only way in which change can be achieved is through learning. The only way learning can develop is through action. By doing nothing, there is no learning and therefore no change regardless of whether the action would have produced positive or negative results.

There is a distinct relationship between the success of a trader and his or her ability to take action, whether the actions turn out to have been right or wrong. Traders who make decisions promptly and without fear, *after* their indicators or systems tell them what to do, most often come out ahead in the long run. Although seemingly paradoxical, it has also been my observation that there is an inverse correlation between intellectual ability and market success—the smarter you are (or think you are), the more you think, and the less money you make.

I am not saying that you have to be stupid or ignorant in order to trade successfully. What I am saying, however, is that you cannot overanalyze a trade or you will either be too late to make the trade or you talk yourself out of it. Traders who can act quickly, evaluating information and reacting to it on an action level, are often traders who succeed. Note that I am not advocating irrational or impulsive behavior. I am saying that *once the facts are in, they are in*—and action is the next step.

What Inhibits Action?

The fear of being wrong inhibits action. But if this is the fear that keeps you from making decisions, then you had better give up the game—there is no way you can play the game without taking some degree of fear. You never know ahead of time whether your decision will be profitable or not. If you did, then there would be no game. There would be no losers to help sustain the winners.

The key antidote for fear is confidence. Confidence comes from having valid and effective systems and methods. Lack of confidence in trading is not usually the result of a psychological or behavioral disorder. It is a lack of confidence in your methodology. Simply stated, the development and application of profitable methods build confidence. Confidence trumps fear.

Feelings Are Not Facts!

Have you observed a relationship between your feelings about a given trade and its eventual success or failure? Consider this: The more a trade scares you, the more likely it is to be successful. The ones you are scared out of are often the ones that work. Why? The human brain cannot function in a vacuum. It needs information to process. If you feed it information that is not factual but that appears to be factual, then the brain reaches erroneous conclusions that are based on feelings and not facts!

Trade—Do Not Overthink!

Blunders are more plentiful than winning behaviors. Consider the following list of blunders, which are ordinarily considered the byproduct of "informed" thought. Consider how much money you have lost or failed to make as a result of these opinions disguised as facts:

- *There is too much risk.* This is basically an excuse for fear. It is been said, "You do not know how deep a hole is until you stand in it." This applies to the risk of trading as well. If it is the degree of dollar risk that is bothering you then there are many ways in which this problem may be resolved or mitigated. Risk can be decreased by the use of futures options and/or options strategies. Risk evaluation is an intangible. If intangibles scare you, then do not drive a car. If you really think about what could happen to you on an expressway then you will not want to drive. If you think about the risk of trading, then you will not trade.
- *I do not feel good about this trade—it scares me.* Here is a favorite cop out on the list of excuses. Assuming that your signal to trade came from a computer or from a mechanical trading system, then your excuse is without merit. Your computer had no idea that you do not like the trade. Nor does the computer care about your feelings. Following feelings or "the force" may have been good for Luke Skywalker, but it is a totally bogus approach when signals come from a mechanical system or a computer.
- *The trade looks good but.* Here is a worthless bit of reasoning. The signal looks good but ... But what? You want to get in cheaper... you want to wait for a pullback ... you want more confirmation... you want to wait for a report... you want to wait for the next signal... you want to talk to your broker first... *Excuses*... all poor excuses, which are the bastard child of what you think is good thinking! You might as well wait to ask your dead grandfather if the trade is good.
- *Let's see how the market opens before I enter my order.* Check it after the first hour of trading. Put in an order below the market above the market. Here is an excuse that I have used hundreds of times. Trading is primarily a game of stimulus and response. The signal is your stimulus and you must make the proper response.
- *Perhaps I'll trade a spread or an option instead.* This bit of thinking is certainly a more creative one, possibly even an intellectual thought. But

it is totally wrong! Entering a spread as an alternative to a flat position is like entering a spread to avoid taking a loss. One action has nothing to do with the other. It is like giving peanut butter to a man dying of thirst.

- *And last, but by no means less absurd, is the "It just doesn't look right" excuse.* This one comes from truly deep thought. It comes from an analysis of the economy, trends, possibly even volume and open interest, and of course, from the input of too many traders and advisors. It you want to get totally confused and frozen into inaction think about—all the facts and opinions, evaluate them all, throw them into the hopper, and decide that you can't decide because something does not seem right. Here is the real thinking trader's excuse. And it is another totally worthless one.

We Are *All* Far from Perfect

Do not think for even one second that I am preaching to you from a position of perfection. I have made more than my share of mistakes. And I will continue to make mistakes for as long as I live. I hope that I will make fewer mistakes and less serious ones as I go along, which is my hope for you as well.

Try a little experiment. Make a commitment to take the next ten trades without thinking about them. After you have done so evaluate your results. See how you have done. See how you feel. Here is what I think you will find: you have spent less valuable time on meaningless thought; you have made the trades you were supposed to make; you will feel better about yourself—more confident and more secure—and you have probably made money as well.

Why We Can't Always Learn from Our Losses

The late and great American learning psychologists have given us great insights into how people learn and how they forget. Perhaps the greatest contribution that psychologists like behaviorist B. F. Skinner made was to show us that most of our emotional responses are not innate but rather learned. As traders, we can learn a great deal about the learning process by studying what these eminent psychologists have discovered. The lessons learned apply to all traders and all systems. Whether you are trading seasonals, cycles, fundamentals, or mechanical systems it is imperative that you learn from every loss you take. Losses are the tuition you pay for your education in the markets.

While we are born with the capacity to feel certain emotions, it is our relationship with the environment (which we call "learning") that attaches certain emotions to certain events. Very often the emotional attachments we connect to certain events are illogical or, what traditional psychiatrists have termed "neurotic."

E. L. Thorndike, was the "father" of American learning psychology. He was among the first to suggest that we learn emotional responses. He also noted that there are literally thousands of "wrong" behaviors we can learn and only a relatively few "right" behaviors.

How can we "unlearn" nonproductive or bad behaviors and replace them with productive, good behaviors? How can a trader overcome losing ways and replace them with winning ways? Can reward and punishment be used as motivators? Why? Do not we learn much from our trading losses? These are some of the important issues that learning psychologists can answer for us.

Thorndike pointed out that although parents and educators have used punishment for many years, it is only effective in specific circumstances and is virtually ineffective in teaching new behaviors when used alone. If I punish you every time you do a particular thing I do not like, you will stop doing that thing. However, you may still do many other things that I do not like.

I can punish you for each and every behavior I wish you to eliminate but my battle may be a life-long one akin to picking dandelions from my lawn without removing the roots. While some new behaviors may be taught with punishment, the use of rewards for appropriate behaviors gets faster, better, and longer-lasting results.

- Consider the ramifications for education, effective child-rearing, and personal development.
- Consider the ramifications for positive interpersonal relationships.
- Consider the ramifications for the trader and investor.

Yes, there are literally hundreds of behaviors and variations on the themes of these behaviors, which can lead to losses. But there are few behaviors and their themes that can facilitate trading success. The unfortunate fact is that most traders are prisoners of their faulty early childhood education and are therefore prisoners of their ineffective trading behaviors as well.

There are many ways to lose money in the markets, but there are only a few ways to make money. And there are even fewer ways to keep money. While traders collectively spend millions of dollars every year attending seminars, buying books, tapes, and trading systems, they focus very little energy on learning the behaviors that will facilitate success. Why? Because the rules of trading systems, methods and indicators are very specific, often objective, and frequently require nothing more than rote memorization. In other words, they are easy to learn and easy to apply.

Behaviors, which contribute to success, on the other hand, are often intangible, but without a plan, you cannot be successful in isolating these behaviors. All you can learn without a plan is what may not work, not what does work!

If you trade without a plan, your chances of success are slim to none. Yes, you may be one of the lucky few who hit it big the first time, but the odds are minimal. Without a plan, you will find yourself buffeted about by the winds of chance, the opinions of others, the persuasion of newsletters and advisors, the pressures of fast-talking brokers and the bias of the media. Your responses will be whimsical. *But the greatest danger is that you will not learn anything from your behavior.*

If you are unaware of what you did wrong, the consequences of your actions will not be deadly apparent to you. And you may run out of money before you learn your lessons. But what exactly do I mean by a "plan?"

Here is my definition of a trading plan:

> *a set of indicators that will permit relatively objective evaluation of market entry and exit as well as risk management.*

This could mean that you are following a computerized trading system from a chart book, a newsletter, astrology, or a random number generator. Regardless of where the input comes from, it must be treated as relatively closely as possible and as often as possible. What I recommend is that you employ a relatively mechanical trade entry system and a more flexible exit system. In other words, I advise against rigidity, against inflexibility following any plan. But to stray from a play, you must have a plan at the outset.

There are various levels of adherence to a plan. Every trader must find his or her level of comfort in straying from the beaten path. Some traders feel uncomfortable with just a minor deviation from the course and others are able to tolerate wide variances with their plans. The final determinant must be your results in the marketplace.

Here are some ways to increase your odds of *losing* money. This is the reverse psychology of trading:

1. *Subscribe to and read as many publications as you can, watch the television business news and follow the consensus of opinion, and get as much information as possible off the Internet.* This is a surefire way to get confused and lose money while you are doing it. You will find that most of your best trades are not only contrary to what you have read, but also contrary to what you want to believe. If you follow a trading advisor, do so without second-guessing. Remember that the more opinions you process, the more confused you will get.

2. *Start with a very small amount of capital and build it up.* Wrong! The facts show that the less you start with, the less likely your odds are of success. If you do not have enough capital to sit through a string of losses, you will not be there to get in on the big winner when it finally comes.
3. *Try to pick tops and bottoms.* This is another surefire way to lose money. Tops and bottoms do not happen too often. Trying to pick them is like trying to find a needle in a haystack. You can find seasonal lows and highs with a good degree of success. However, you are always best getting into existing trends and riding them. You are better off trading with the established trend as opposed to trying to pick a change in trend before it happens.
4. *Get out of your winners quickly and ride your losers.* Many traders get anxious when they are in profitable positions. They have the urge to take the money and run before the market takes it back from them. But when they are in a losing position they are patient and remorseful. They get mesmerized into a state of no action, hoping that the market will reverse the trend. They ride losses for a long time and exit profits quickly. This is another good way to lose money in the markets.
5. *Buy a better trading system.* It is not the system that makes profits—it is the trader. In the hand of a poor trader, a good system is useless. Spend more time developing yourself as opposed to your system and it will be time well spent. Simple and inexpensive systems often work best. Every now and then you will run across an expensive system that holds promise. If you decide to buy it and if you are convinced it is worthwhile, you must also make the commitment to trade it according to the rules. If you cannot do that, do not waste your money on the system.
6. *Spread your position to avoid taking a loss.* This little trick rarely works. In fact, it most often puts you into double jeopardy. It is just another way to generate commissions and losses.
7. *Get into trading for the action.* Most traders do not understand themselves. In fact, most traders are uncertain about their goals in the market. They will tell you that they are looking for profits, but their behavior will convey another message. Many traders trade just for the action. Some traders enjoy telling their friends that they speculate in futures." And yet, other traders trade just to legally satisfy a need to gamble.

   Some traders trade just for the challenge. Although there is probably nothing wrong with most of these goals, the fact is that most traders do not know that these are, in fact, their goals. They do not understand their motivation and, in failing to do so, they cannot direct their intellectual energy in the appropriate direction. Self-understanding facilitates attainment of goals by highlighting the best vehicle toward the desired end.

Furthermore, the failure to understand one's self will obscure the reasons for losses. Hence, the learning process is either slowed down or totally ineffective. Since it is the function of losses to educate, the value of losses will not be fully effective if it is at all beneficial.

8. *Believe that risk is for other traders.* It would appear that there are many trading systems, methods and timing indicators that have profit potential. Those of us who have developed and tested trading systems know that although profitable systems are not easy to find, they *do exist.* But, as the Zen philosopher said, "Every front has a back and the bigger the back, the bigger the front." Simply stated, every trading system, no matter how well it performs in hypothetical testing, has its downside.

   The greater the rewards promised by the system, the greater the risk exposure. The simple fact of the matter is that trading involves risk and that there is no system, method or indicator that has ever been developed which does not entail risk. We accept this as a fact of trading life. As strange as this may sound to you, many traders do not understand the true meaning of risk. They feel that risk is for other traders. Only when controlled with the reality of risk and loss do they understand its full impact. Only when the threat of loss is real can they respond.

9. *Trade without the skills necessary to implement a trading system effectively, systematically, and in a disciplined fashion.* After years of study, I have concluded that trading systems, methods, and indicators constitute perhaps 23 percent of the total equation for success, 15 percent is luck, and the remaining 60 percent depends on trader response to the system and the markets. All traders are not created equal when it comes to trading discipline. Some are more reactive than others are, some more tense than others are, some are too confident, others too sensitive, and others too detached.

   It is the response of the trader that constitutes the single most important variable in the equation for trading success. Too many traders lose in the futures markets simply because they do not possess the necessary skills to trade effectively.

Implementation Is the Key to Everything!

When I was a practicing psychologist, I helped many patients achieve great insights into their behavior. I helped them understand the whys and wherefores of their behaviors. But these understandings, unless followed by actions, were nothing more than romantic exercises.

There are traders who spend hours and hours developing systems that appear to have great profit potential—systems that back test beautifully, but that remain nothing more than works of art, never traded due to the fear or indolence of their developer.

Once you have pinpointed the reasons that you have failed to realize your full potential, you must act immediately or the opportunity will be lost. You will fail to seize the opportunity and time will be lost. The longer you wait the less capable you will be of taking action because a lack of action will become comfortable to you. For all of the many ways to lose in the market, the key to reversing the trend is to take action and implement your plan for success.

IN CLOSING

The lessons in this book have been drawn from my more than 35 years of experience as a trader, market analyst, educator, and observer of trader behavior. I have designed them to be specific and as objective as possible. But the lessons would not have been complete without a section on the weakest part of the trading sequence—the trader. I hope that my experiences and the methods I have developed will prove useful or better yet, profitable to you.

Should you have questions, comments, or suggestions, please write to me at jake@trade-futures.com.

Index

Page numbers followed by an *f* indicate figures.
Page numbers followed by an *t* indicate tables.